THE CASE AGAINST
THE
ESTABLISHMENT

NICK ADAMS
with Dave Erickson

Post Hill
PRESS

A POST HILL PRESS BOOK
ISBN: 978-1-68261-474-7
ISBN (eBook): 978-1-68261-475-4

The Case Against the Establishment
© 2017 by Nick Adams
All Rights Reserved

Cover art by Dan Pitts

Post Hill Press
New York • Nashville
posthillpress.com

Published in the United States of America

To the risk-takers, rule-breakers, and game-changers. And to the country that gives those people a home—America. Finally, to the American people who have embraced me in a way the people of my native country never did.

TABLE OF CONTENTS

FOREWORD

A linchpin is a small metal pin that, seen or unseen, keeps a wheel on its axis. Geopolitically, America is the free world's linchpin—the "central cohesive source of support and stability" that serves as an indispensable, if imperfect, beacon of freedom in a dangerous world.

But the linchpin is vulnerable. Without long-overdue reforms and intentional education, and absent core principles, America could soon become a European welfare state—less prosperous at home and more impotent overseas—making the world a far more chaotic, and less free, place.

America's culture, economy, and political system have resiliencies that other world powers have lacked—but none make America immune from the trend lines of history. American conservatives must rejuvenate conservatism (Americanism!), thereby renewing America's promise at home and abroad.

This is not an easy task, and will mean confronting long-established entrenched interests at home and rearming to face eminent threats abroad. Only a strong America—economically at home and militarily abroad—will ensure that the twenty-first century is an American century.

These are things that Nick Adams, a patriotic superstar, has understood his entire life. It's why he couldn't wait to immigrate to this country and become an American. He understands that "Establishment" equals gatekeepers. He knows that the Establishment delivers crushing blows to opportunity. The Establishment serves itself, not America.

That is why this book, *The Case Against the Establishment,* is an incredibly important work and a must-read for all patriotic Americans. It lays out the case against all those seeking to weaken America by removing the American exceptionalism that has made our country the indispensable linchpin of humankind. God bless America and this great book!

Pete Hegseth
Fox News contributor and US Army veteran

INTRODUCTION

Establishment: an established order of society: such as (a) a group of social, economic, and political leaders who form a ruling class (as of a nation); (b) a controlling group.

–Merriam-Webster's Collegiate® Dictionary, 11th Edition
© 2017 by Merriam-Webster, Inc.

To make a case against the Establishment, which we're obligated to do because, frankly, that's the title of the book, we must define Establishment. *Merriam-Webster* did a nice job. Succinct. To the point. Sure, the Establishment is a ruling class. Yep, it's a controlling group. But one would figure the scapegoat for every political ill in America must be so much more than that. Come on, in this political climate, the term "Establishment" is more ubiquitous than snowflakes at a Trump protest. Simply put . . .

The Establishment is the enemy of the people.

And forget the proverb about "the enemy of my enemy"— when it comes to the Establishment, the enemy of my enemy is *not* my friend, because even the anti-Establishment *is* the Establishment. Grab a freedom fry and read on, we'll explain in a minute.

The Establishment *hates* American exceptionalism. It finds abhorrent the belief the United States has a special calling, a divine purpose, and stands above every other nation on Earth. For them, "patriotism" is spelled with four letters. National pride? Shame is what it's called. Let's send our president on an "apology tour." The Establishment worldview is a fixed worldview where to question it invites mockery and to embrace it, acceptance. Conformity is king and individualism nonexistent.

The immediate and fundamental goal of the Establishment is to remake the United States of America into the European Union. Inconsequential borders and no national identities. A vast community of sheeple full of peace, love, and understanding, singing "Kumbaya," and ruled by an elite few. How's that working out? Can you say "Brexit"? The people of Great Britain had had enough, said "Toddle Pip," and voted to leave, leaving Establishment elites with their knickers in a twist. Have national pride? You're a xenophobe. Refugees without vetting? Come on in! Exceptional? Not important. Hopefully, Emmanuel Macron shares his Beef Bourguignon with the less fortunate because, ya know, socialists always pay their fair share.

If any of this sounds like the American left, you've got a great ear because they're pretty much the same. By being Establishment you must have left-wing positions. Yeah, we're looking at you too, RINOs.

Border security? Who needs it?! Those poor dreamers illegally crossing our borders need our provision. We've got $100 billion we can spend on them every year, no problem.

Let's tax hardworking Americans and use their money to provide those ~~criminals~~ immigrants with health care and a college education. The homeless American veterans living on the streets, they'll be fine.

The Establishment embraces multiculturalism but truth be told, the greatness of multiculturalism ends with the food. Have you ever tried oven-fried pork carnitas with guacamole and orange salsa? It is to die for.

The Establishment considers itself the engine and the American people the spokes and the wheels. It wants a society of lemmings. Independent thought? That's a hate crime. Free speech? Only if your viewpoint mirrors theirs exactly, otherwise you're likely a racist, a fascist, or a Nazi. If you're a Trump supporter, congratulations, you're all three!

Led by the Hollywood elite, the Establishment has launched a visual and aural onslaught of hate and hypocrisy the likes of which we've not seen since, well, Nazi Germany. Ironic, isn't it? It's the Establishment squashing free speech and using violence to silence opposing viewpoints. Hmm, isn't that what fascists do?

The Establishment is hypocrisy.

Matt Damon can say with a straight face that he wants America to ban guns, while reaping millions of dollars from films in which he's killing people with . . . guns.

Leonardo DiCaprio talks about the importance of environmental responsibility. The man flies in private jets with carbon footprints bigger than Sean Penn's ego.

Pope Francis, criticizing then-candidate Donald Trump, tells journalists a person who thinks about building walls, wherever they may be, is not a Christian. The Pontiff lives in a country, Vatican City, surrounded by a forty-foot wall.

Hypocrisy thy name is Establishment.

Meanwhile, the Establishment news media has abandoned all pretense of objectivity. It's simply a runaway locomotive of propaganda. The halcyon days of anti-American Establishment leadership came to an end, their anointed successor lost despite their best efforts, and now it's seek and destroy, divide and conquer. Half of the country is made up of lemmings, the other half, proud "deplorables" who know better.

Also, Russians.

If you believe the Establishment media, Russia is run by the diabolical Vladimir Putin in his underground bunker manipulating American presidential elections.

But all this Establishment maneuvering, as far-reaching as it is, is single-minded of purpose: to keep Donald Trump from his self-appointed task of making America great again.

He won and that just pisses them off. The Establishment has contempt for Middle America. But Middle America showed them. It voted in droves for the one candidate who deliberately and accurately took measures to snatch the power from the Establishment and give it back to the people.

So where *does* President Donald J. Trump fit into all this Establishment talk? He doesn't and that's the point. Constitutional zealots like the Freedom Caucus and Ted Cruz and Rand Paul and others who fancy themselves as anti-Establishment are, in truth, their own Establishment. Regardless of viewpoint, you must subscribe to a certain ideology, have

4

a certain demeanor. Trump is neither of these establishments. He is his own man, which gives him flexibility and appeal, and it carried him all the way to 1600 Pennsylvania Avenue.

SECTION 1

HOW TO BECOME PRESIDENT

CHAPTER 1

HOW DID HE DO IT?

*Congratulations to @realdonaldtrump
for validating hard work in the face of
impossible obstacles, against all odds, with
no experience and only relying on your
own self-belief, native instincts and a show
up–dominate attitude even when the deck
was stacked against you . . . . This is a win
for America reminding all of us no dream is
too big and no obstacle too high. Your win
proves anyone can do anything.*

–Grant Cardone
Business innovator/Renowned sales trainer

How did a billionaire with a penchant for PR and zero political credentials knock off a near-impenetrable monolith like the Establishment? Donald Trump's positions vis-à-vis the GOP seemed dubious at best. His Twitter feed appeared as a Red Bull–fueled stream of consciousness. His rhetoric like gasoline on a still-smoldering fire.

The Establishment never saw it coming. Even as the first election returns were trickling in, they still didn't know what was hitting them, and couldn't comprehend the sheer force of the beating. Ronda Rousey never saw Holly Holm's foot either in UFC 193, but when it hit her in the face, Rousey landed exactly where the Establishment did on Election Night . . . on the floor in a heap of battered flesh. That's what happens when the power elite dismisses a perceived lesser adversary. Trump's foot hit the Establishment in the head, left them beaten and bloodied, and stumbling around wondering just how this political "nobody" could have kicked their butt so soundly.

He beat Hillary Clinton, the anointed one, the cornerstone of Establishment liberals, and before that, sixteen other Republicans. Take a breath and let that number digest.

Sixteen.

Trump's victory was quintessentially American. One man, outgunned, outspent, against the odds, and challenging a dominant foe. Remember the 1980 United States Olympic hockey team and the "Miracle on Ice"? Yep, like that. The only thing missing on Election Night was Al Michaels' play-by-play, "Do you believe in miracles? Yes!"

But that celebrated victory against the Soviet Union was as much about ideology as it was about hockey. Trump's victory wasn't all ideological, it was visceral too. A pundit can blather all day about the value of experience inside the Beltway, but at the end of the day, after eight years of divisive rhetoric and even worse policy, sometimes all a voter wants is an outsider who makes them feel good about the future again.

Enter Donald Trump.

Working-class people across the country—in flyover states, in Rust Belt states, and in Bible Belt states—who felt ignored or dismissed and oft-insulted by the Establishment gravitated toward the person who they *felt* cared about them and the country. Here was a guy who didn't sound like any other politician they'd ever heard. In fact, he *wasn't* a politician. Trump was just a guy who *said* the things they were *thinking*. And the things he said, at least for them, proved he listened.

Incredibly, the mogul and reality television star became a populist hero.

Then there was the ideology . . .

The wall.

Repeal Obamacare.

Lower taxes.

Create jobs.

Destroy ISIS.

Support Israel.

So deep did this message resonate with millions of people that nine and a half months before the election, Trump could say at a campaign stop in Sioux City, Iowa, "The polls, they say I have the most loyal people. Did you ever see that? Where I could stand in the middle of Fifth Avenue and shoot somebody and I wouldn't lose any voters, okay? It's like, incredible," and it be a true statement.

The Establishment hated this guy, and still does. Elites ensconced in urban bastions of Establishment-thinking despised Trump and his supporters. Hillary Clinton said they belonged in a "basket of deplorables." Establishment media went after Trump like he was Nixon and G. Gordon Liddy was streaking through the Rose Garden.

Weeks before the election, they dredged up an eleven-year-old tape from *Access Hollywood*, a show owned by NBC, which painted an unflattering picture of the renegade spoiler poised to deny Hillary the crown. Sexually offensive comments will do that. But Americans saw through the media's faux outrage. Anyone who voted for Bill Clinton and still revels in his "greatness" forfeits any credibility to claim offense at Trump's words. Lest we forget, the forty-second president of the United States used a twenty-two-year-old intern as a human humidor for his big Gurkha.

Establishment media unleashed often-baseless attacks disguised as journalism and a new buzz phrase entered the zeitgeist: "fake news." They conducted stilted polls aimed at demoralizing Trump's base. If the polls show he has no chance to win, then they won't vote. But the Establishment media forgot one important thing: the only polls that matter are the ones on Election Day.

On that day, America had two choices. Well, okay, there were four choices, but Gary Johnson and Dr. Jill Stein, really? On November 8, 2016, half the people in this country had a sinking feeling, like Howard Beale, the mad prophet of the airwaves in the Paddy Chayefsky masterpiece film *Network*, that we knew things were bad, worse than bad—they're crazy! And on Election Day the only thing left for any of us to do was to get up from our chair, go to the window, open it, stick our head out, and yell, "I'm as mad as hell, and I'm not going to take this anymore!"

Or we could go to the polls and vote.

And *that* is how Donald Trump became president of the United States.

CHAPTER 2

YOU CAN'T BE PRESIDENT. NO, SERIOUSLY. YOU CAN'T.

To every little girl who dreams big: yes, you can be anything you want—even president.

– Hillary Clinton
Twitter post, June 7, 2016

Hillary Clinton was the first female in American history to be a major party's nominee for president of the United States.

The accomplishment serves as an inspiration for scores of people seeking dreams seemingly beyond their grasp. People facing federal indictment now have a shining beacon on which to gaze when they wonder whether they too can achieve the American Dream.

People who run sham charities financed by foreign governments can now aspire to hold the highest office in the land!

When Hillary Clinton won the Democratic Party nomination she took to Twitter: "To every little girl who dreams big: yes, you can be anything you want—even president." What a wonderful thing to say. What a wonderful message. What an inspirational mantra.

What a lie.

No little girl, no little boy, no average American woman, no average American man for that matter, has any hope whatsoever of ever becoming president of the United States. And that is exactly how the Establishment wants it.

Fund-raisers who specialize in this sort of thing estimate it costs a couple of billion dollars to win the presidency. Now, I've got a deep sofa, but even I can't find that much money lodged between the cushions. I did find some potato chips though, so there's that.

That's why in 2016, our primary choice to lead the country was between a woman who talks about income inequality while wearing a twelve thousand dollar Armani coat, and an anti-Establishment billionaire.

"Real" people, without access to billions of dollars, cannot become president of the United States.

It's unfortunate because real people were running, but you just didn't know about them. According to the Federal Election Commission, roughly 1,800 people filed to run for president in the 2016 election. Even after you separated the wheat from the chaff among those 1,800, the crackpots from the candidates with something to say, that still left a lot of people not named Trump or Clinton.

You've probably never heard of Robert Macleod Jr. Looking like a guy straight from the casting room of *Duck Dynasty*, he was the "Uncle Si" of the 2016 campaign. A proud, gray beard–wearing, hardworking mechanic by trade, a dyed-in-the-wool American patriot by blood. "I am not a Republican. I am not a Democrat. I am not an Independent. I am an American," was Macleod's mantra. He lived in a town called Americus. Seriously. You get can't much more red, white, and blue than that.

How about Temperance Lance-Council? She was the self-proclaimed "anti-hypocrisy candidate" who fashioned herself not so much as a politician but as a "poli-acto" (short for politician-actress), like Senator Al Franken and the late Senator Fred Thompson. She founded the Anti-Hypocrisy Party to, as she says, "fight back against politicians talking out of both sides of their mouths." Lance-Council has run for president every election year since 2000. Her catchphrase? "You didn't land on Wall Street; Wall Street landed on you!" I have absolutely no clue what that means. Maybe things would have been different had she gone with "Make America Great Again."

Over in Myrtle Beach, South Carolina, where anyone in a thong bikini is an outlaw, and cannabis stokes the passions of men so idealistic they believe it'll one day take us back to space, you'd have found Libertarian candidate Keenan Wallace Dunham. This self-described Mensa high-IQ genius scientist wants to colonize the moon, abolish the IRS, legalize and tax marijuana sales, and use revenue from cannabis to pay for space colonization and to trigger an industrial revolution.

That's quite the aggressive agenda.

Okay, so maybe that's not an agenda for the masses, and Macleod, Lance-Council, and Dunham weren't the candidates for the masses. But there were well more than a thousand others from which to choose. Contrary to what an Establishment system of politics would have you believe, most of those people weren't crackpots chasing a Pollyanna dream. They knew they had no chance, not in a rigged system, anyway. And that's a shame.

What these citizen politicians are doing when they run, right there at the grassroots, is eliciting conversation, thought, and new ways to look at the same issues—something you can't find in an Establishment that lauds backbiting, party infighting, back room deals, and cronyism.

This country needs more *Mr. Smith Goes to Washington* and less *Scandal*.

So, the next time you hear someone say if you work hard enough, you can be president of the United States, tell them, "I'd love to run but that's an Establishment lie. Meantime, I'm voting for the reelection of Donald Trump or maybe that guy who wants to use weed to put us back on the moon."

SECTION 2

WHO AM I?

CHAPTER 3

THE ESTABLISHMENT: WHERE MEN ARE MEN AND SO ARE WOMEN

Caitlyn Jenner Cuts It Off

–The Daily Caller
Twitter headline, April 12, 2017

When there's actual debate about whether someone with a penis should use the men's room and someone with a vagina should use the ladies' room and whether it's inappropriate for the person with a penis to use the ladies' room and whether someone who disagrees with that person using the ladies' room is a misanthrope, then the Establishment has sunk discourse in this country to a new degree of lunacy.

And few things encapsulate as boldly the twisted ideology of Establishment gender politics as the emasculation of American Olympic hero Bruce Jenner.

This man, and make no mistake, a man is exactly what he is (yay, science!), went from the front of a Wheaties cereal box to the front of *Vanity Fair* magazine because the Establishment decided Jenner was the one person, an American icon, it could use to legitimize yet another one of its off-the-wall creeds to further chip away the traditional values most Americans hold dear.

You know the Jenner story. After years of struggling with his gender identity, in 2015 the decathlon gold medalist from the Games of the XXI Olympiad told the world, both in a heralded ABC interview with Diana Sawyer and a *Vanity Fair* cover story, that he was a woman trapped in a man's body and was in the process of transitioning from "Bruce" to "Caitlyn." Then in January of 2017, according to Jenner's memoir, *The Secrets of My Life*, he made the transition complete by undergoing gender reassignment surgery. Yep, as the *Daily Caller* proclaimed, Caitlyn cut it off.

By most accounts, Bruce/Caitlyn is a good person and, to the Establishment's horror, a declared Republican who admits to voting for Donald Trump. Egads! So, the issue isn't with someone who clearly had a personal struggle, it's with an Establishment that would mainstream this type of thinking— that sex and gender aren't the same thing. The Establishment tells you the individual determines gender. If you don't like being a man or a woman you can "identify" as something else.

In the fall of 2016, the *New Atlantis: A Journal of Technology and Society*, published its findings from a comprehensive study they hoped would "offer some *scientific* insight about the mental health issues faced by LGBT populations." (emphasis added)

What the *New Atlantis* found destroys the Establishment narrative like a MOAB destroys an ISIS tunnel.

In a report entitled "Sexuality and Gender: Findings from the Biological, Psychological, and Social Sciences," they concluded, "The hypothesis that gender identity is an innate, fixed property of human beings that is independent of biological sex—that a person might be 'a man trapped in a woman's body' or 'a woman trapped in a man's body'—is not supported by scientific evidence."

Boom! (insert mic drop here)

Biology determines gender.

Imagine that. People born with boy parts are boys and people born with girl parts are girls.

You can't argue with science, but try they do.

The Establishment denies the science of sexual identity while simultaneously chastising global warming skeptics as "science deniers." They never see the patterns of their own hypocrisy. This is a prevalent theme with the Establishment. They force-feed their views to the masses, and anyone who dares to reject them is subject to name-calling, in this case, called an ignorant transphobe. However, the only ignorance here is with the people who don't know the definition of the word "phobic." A person isn't afraid, nay phobic, for believing science and not emotion dictates gender.

It's also not phobic to find it three klicks west of crazy *Glamour* magazine's decision to name Caitlyn Jenner as one of its 2015 "Women of the Year." You'd think it rational to surmise that anyone with a twig and berries wouldn't qualify for such an honor, but rational isn't typically the Establishment's way.

In 2016, the Williams Institute, a think tank at the UCLA School of Law, issued a report estimating that fewer than 1 percent of American adults identify as transgender in the United States; a minuscule 0.6 percent

0.6 percent.

Yet, the Establishment pushes its ideology on the masses as though *they're* the norm. It demands the rest of us, which is *most* of us, kowtow to accommodate their view. That's why you have a mega-retailer like Target instituting a policy that allows transgender people to use whichever restroom matches their gender identity and alienating families by effectively saying, "Hey, go ahead, use whichever restroom matches the gender with which you identify. Sure, Chester, you can use the ladies' room, no problem!"

Protest the policy, the Establishment eviscerates you. A parent concerned their daughter might end up in a bathroom with a man pretending to identify as a woman? They're puritanical and intolerant! Never mind the reports of "peeping Toms" taking pictures or shooting video inside Target bathrooms and fitting rooms.

But what the Establishment never prepares for is the mettle of real Americans. You saw it with the election of Donald Trump. People revolted against the Establishment by electing him president, and they revolted against the Target bathroom policy by boycotting the store chain. The publically traded company's stock value took a "yuge" hit. Target, which has about 1,800 stores, later pledged to spend $20 million to put private bathrooms in the 300 stores that didn't already have them.

Despite the consequences, the Establishment never ends its quest to make transgenderism a mainstream thing. It hates America's traditional values, and those who dare to uphold them are worthy of destruction. Don't believe it? Ask North Carolina.

In early 2016, the state passed House Bill 2, more commonly known as HB2, which put clear and concise limits on single-sex, multiple occupancy bathroom and changing facilities in schools and public agencies. The bill required people using multiple-occupancy facilities like school bathrooms, locker rooms, dressing rooms, and so forth to match the biological sex listed on their birth certificate. What?! Well, that's just prosaic! Try as the Establishment may to convince us otherwise, no parent wants their little girl in a bathroom with a grown man. And certainly, no woman wants to be in a locker room under the watchful eye of Generalissimo Weenis.

In North Carolina, public safety and privacy still matter to most people, unless you're the Establishment, then forcing a minority position matters more. A policy that protects kids? Seek and destroy. The Establishment launched an onslaught of hate at North Carolina. The talking heads and headlines said it all. If you believed them, the state was populated by nothing but transphobes, homophobes, and close-minded rubes.

What the Establishment failed to tell most people was the bill *did* provide for the accommodation of the transgendered.

HB2 specifically stated, "Nothing in this section shall prohibit local boards of education from providing accommodations such as single occupancy bathroom or changing facilities or controlled use of faculty facilities upon a request due to special circumstances." Most people never knew that because the Establishment banks on most people never actually reading a bill or doing their own research. Instead it preys on emotion. The lemmings fall for it every time.

The furor even triggered the NCAA to snatch back seven championship events already awarded to North Carolina for 2016–2017. In its statement announcing the decision, the NCAA claimed the reason for doing so was "because of the cumulative actions taken by the state concerning civil rights protections." Civil rights protections? Did the person who came up with the statement do it with a straight face? Just one month after pulling the events from North Carolina, Stanford and Harvard's men's basketball teams played a game in Shanghai, China. Civil rights protections are so important to the NCAA, it stood back while the Pac-12 conference sanctioned a game in a country with one of the poorest records for human rights in the world.

And just one month before the two-faced NCAA ripped millions of dollars from the North Carolina economy, Louisville and Bowling Green became the first women's college basketball programs to ever play in Cuba.

Wait, what?

Cuba?!

So, to the NCAA, North Carolina is a bigger affront than Cuba, whose citizens have suffered some of the worst abuses of human rights on Earth.

How do you fight that kind of thinking?

Establishment thinking is illogical.

Establishment thinking is hypocritical.

Establishment thinking is anti-American.

Establishment thinking is two transgender employees of the University of Wisconsin suing because the university's health insurance plan refuses to pay for gender-reassignment surgery.

Establishment thinking is putting signs that say "gender-free" outside single-occupancy public bathrooms, which was an actual proposal in the Vermont House of Representatives.

Establishment thinking is Facebook listing more than fifty gender identities from which to choose.

Establishment thinking is the Texas legislature battling over its own bathroom bill, worried about the same repercussions suffered by North Carolina.

Oh, and HB2? It's dead. Sort of. Less than a year after passing it, North Carolina capitulated to the Establishment and passed a bill repealing it. But the new bill did leave enough of the old bill intact for the Establishment bullies to maintain their place on the pulpit.

But here's the thing—no matter how hard it pushes, at the end of the day, the one thing the Establishment can never beat with its arguments is biology. Truth is, cutting off your penis doesn't make you a woman, it just makes you a man without a penis.

Sorry, man, it's science.

CHAPTER 4

WHAT'S YOUR FAVORITE COLOR?

*Just as a transgender person might be
born male but identify as female, I wasn't
pretending to be something I wasn't but
expressing something I already was. I
wasn't passing as Black; I was Black, and
there was no going back.*

–Rachel Dolezal
*In Full Color: Finding My Place in a
Black and White World*

In the Establishment worldview, race and gender are never absolute. If you're white, you can be black. If you're black, you can be white. If you're male, you can be female. If you're female, you can be male. If *you* believe that's what you are, then that's what you are!

Rachel Dolezal certainly believes it. For years, the former president of the Spokane, Washington chapter of the NAACP, successfully convinced people she was black, though thanks to her parents who outed her in 2015, we learned that underneath the bronzer, Dolezal's whiter than a Dave Matthews concert.

Self-delusion does wonders for self-advancement.

How else to explain it? The Establishment doesn't see the intrinsic irony of a Caucasian deluding herself into thinking she's black, then running a chapter of an organization created for black people. Sure, the NAACP was formed by white people, but as far as we know, none of them claimed to be black.

That the Establishment validates Dolezal's "identity" makes her story a seemingly real-life reverse version of Clayton Bigsby, the black, white supremacist created by comic Dave Chappelle. For his television show in 2003, Chappelle wrote and performed a brilliant PBS *Frontline* parody about a white supremacist named Clayton Bigsby, who, because he was born blind, doesn't know he's black. Bigsby identified as white, so his ~~enablers~~ friends played along—much like the Establishment does with Dolezal. At the end of the bit, Bigsby learns that he is, in fact, black. He ultimately accepts reality, something Dolezal won't.

Like Caitlyn Jenner and the rest of the Establishment, Dolezal has yet to accept that you can't argue with biology. But, oh boy, does she try. In a March 2017 interview with the BBC, Dolezal dropped diatribe so nonsensical it makes Bill Nye look like Einstein. She said, "We've evolved into understanding that gender is not binary, it's not even biological. But what strikes me as so odd is that race isn't biological either. I believe that the word 'transracial' has become socially useful in describing racial fluidity and identity."

Gender *isn't* biological?

Race *isn't* biological?

Is Dolezal insane or just plain stupid?

The idea you can "identify" with whatever race or gender you want to be, then, science be damned, you become it, then the rest of the world must accept it, is an absurdist notion only an Establishmentarian would buy.

Although the rest of us could try to see things from the Establishment perspective. This weekend I'll be identifying as a black woman. I plan to drop my white name and adopt a West African moniker like Dolezal did (Nkechi Amare Diallo), then write a missive for *Vanity Fair à la* Caitlyn Jenner that'll go something like this . . .

I've spent the entirety of my life denying my identity, so here it is . . . I am a black woman trapped in a white man's body.

I'm so happy after such a long struggle to be living my true self.

I know many of you will call me brave, that my coming out is a true act of heroism, and that I'm now in the enviable position of role model and ambassador for others struggling with duality. I never envisioned that, nor was that my aim, but if coming to grips with who I am and being true to myself empowers others toward acceptance, then I wear that mantle proudly.

As a young man dating white women, I always felt uneasy. Dinner parties, cocktail gatherings, get-togethers in my primarily white neighborhood, forced to listen to Nickelback . . . I never felt comfortable. The need to be accepted into societal norms forced me into a cavernous fortress of denial.

It was as though when God created me, He looked down and said, "Okay, what are we going to do with this one?" Make him a smart kid, very determined, and He gave me these wonderful qualities. And at the end, when He's just finishing, He goes, "Wait a second, we gotta give him something. Everybody has stuff in their life that they must deal with, you know? What are we gonna give him?" God looks down and chuckles a little bit and goes, "Hey, let's give him the soul of a black woman and let's see how he deals with that."

I've been confused with my identity ever since. It's just who I am as a human being. My brain is much more black woman than it is white man. It's hard for people to understand that. But that's what my soul is.

Granted there's nothing in me physiologically that says I am black or female, but I believe it, I've declared it, I identify with it, and that's what matters. I truly believe I'm a black woman, so you must believe as well. For anyone who doesn't believe what I believe about myself, regardless of biology, is an unsympathetic, hate-fueled, intolerant miscreant.

Hopefully, I'll be on the cover of next month's Essence, and then I can finally say, "Welcome to the world, black woman, can't wait for you to get to know me."

SECTION 3

THIS IS HIGHER EDUCATION?

CHAPTER 5
ESTABLISHMENT U.

Wussification 101: Examines core concepts of taking offense at everything in society no matter the intent. Focuses on creating adults unable to process life in the real world by using enabling methods and applying "understanding," coddling, and behavior constructs incorporating the assumption of microaggression into every life challenge. *

Establishment University, where courses like Wussification 101 equip young adults for a life of entitlement, victimhood, offense, and narcissism. And nowadays, *every* university is Establishment U. (* No, this is not an actual course.)

Much like the Establishment itself, today's academic landscape breeds intolerance, hate, fascism, anti-American rhetoric, and all manner of intellectual elitism. It's also a harbinger for an ever-expanding class of the spineless.

What the Establishment has raised up is a generation of coddled millennials without the mettle to brave such atrocities as name-calling, Halloween costumes deemed "offensive," or, well, words. These young adults occupy an alternate reality running parallel to actual reality. A couple of generations ago, young adults, kids really, occupied the front lines fighting Nazis. A generation after that, they were in Southeast Asia, knee-deep in rice patties and napalm, dodging snipers, land mines, and all manner of horror. It's unfortunate there wasn't a safe space for them, like the ones today's students need to escape the barbarity of name-calling.

Name-calling.

At the University of Houston, a psychology department adviser, in an undercover video shot by Project Veritas, cited name-calling as just one example of the emotional distress with which UH students must cope. She said students should be able to ask for an "emotional first aid kit" to handle the stress.

Imagine needing an emotional first aid kit to handle the stress of name-calling. I'm sorry this wasn't available when I was in college. I'd have been able to handle it better when that mean fraternity guy called me "Crocodile Dundee."

What the Establishment hasn't taught these students is there's stress in all manner of life, like being a single mother, working two jobs, figuring out how to pay the rent. Stress is raising a special needs child. Stress is having a terminal illness with not enough insurance to cover the cost of treatment. Stress is watching your teenager wrestle with drug addiction. Stress is a shylock threatening to break your fingers because you owe twenty G's to a guy named Momo. Stress is a lot of things, with a lot of causes. What it is not? Being a college kid who is called a name, and it damn sure isn't a mispronounced name.

Yep, that's also a thing. In 2015, a study by the Santa Clara County, California Office of Education and the National Association for Bilingual Education concluded students experience "anxiety and resentment" when a teacher mispronounces their name. I can't imagine what life is like for little Bobby Vagina . . . "It's pronounced, vash-in-ay!"

We've got radical Islamic lunatics setting off pressure cooker bombs in our streets and these people are upset someone mispronounced their name?

How did we arrive here? Absent parents? Lazy parents? Participation ribbons?

Over at California State University, Chico, they took up an educational campaign called "You Don't Say" where it warned students to avoid using certain words and phrases some people might find offensive.

The school, at the urging of its Student-Athlete Advisory Committee (SAAC), put up posters around campus displaying these so-called offensive words and phrases with a warning to avoid using them.

At the time, Haley Kroll, the co-president of SAAC, said, "Everyone is welcome here. We are a family. We want everyone to feel included, and we want our language to reflect that." Yeah, well Kroll is the personification of how our college campuses have turned into little snowflake pastures where nary a coddled sprite should ever need a backbone to brave the barbarity of words.

Phrases like "man up."

See, "man up," on the Chico campus, insinuates women can't be courageous. Really? I always thought it meant "don't be a p*ssy." Oh wait, you can't call someone a p*ssy either, because a part of a woman's body should never be used as a connotation for weakness, at least that's what their poster says.

Now, I'm old school. I get it, or maybe that's why I don't get it. I was raised at a time when my parents and authority figures told me "sticks and stones would break my bones but names would never hurt me." But Establishment authority figures these days indulge the martyr mentality, where everyone is a victim, taking offense at words and phrases determined to be offensive by sheltered elitists occupying college campuses. Run for a safe space, kids, there's rhetoric incoming!

God only knows how any of us over the age of thirty survived high school.

So, who decides when a word is offensive and when a meathead is just being a meathead? Don't we get to decide that for ourselves? If George Carlin told us in the early '70s the most inappropriate words for some were the "seven dirty words you can't say on TV," then who is telling us now we can't say things like . . . "coward"?

At Cal State Chico "coward" is considered offensive because, as their poster says, "You can't judge someone else by your own standards."

Yes, I can! That's what judging is. I can judge by my standards, by the law, by the Constitution, by the Code of Hammurabi, any standard I want, and the standard for cowardice is generally universal—you're being a p*ssy.

Say you're offended by a certain Halloween costume on campus. You can cower in a safe space, or if you attend the

University of Florida, you can follow the school's urging and report the costumes as bias.

Far-fetched? Nope. Just before Halloween in 2016, UF offered up counseling services for students offended by costumes. Let that marinate for a minute. College students taking offense at a Halloween costume? Welcome to Dystopia, check your common sensibilities at the door.

So, if you planned to dress as Captain America next Halloween, forget it. Your costume might be reported for perpetuating a negative stereotype and for insulting someone who found patriotism galling and the national anthem oppressive. Captain America? He's culturally inappropriate!

In an online posting titled "Halloween Costume Choices," the UF administration wrote, "If you choose to participate in Halloween activities, we encourage you to think about your choices of costumes and themes. Some Halloween costumes reinforce stereotypes of particular races, genders, cultures, or religions. Regardless of intent, these costumes can perpetuate negative stereotypes, causing harm and offense to groups of people."

This is the same school where a fraternity once threw a "rock stars and rappers" party and its members showed up in blackface, "bling," and butt-exposing baggy pants. A year before that, one of the school's softball players tweeted a photo from a party where the attendees were dressed as football players in blackface.

Perhaps the genesis of heightened sensitivities is right there, and it begat social justice warriors which begat safe zones which begat BERT, the Bias Education and Response

Team. It's a real thing at the University of Florida. Find offense? Call BERT!

In fact, more than two hundred campuses across the country, both private and public, have some form of a bias response team.

BERT, BERT, he's your man, if he can't coddle you, no one can!

Are you the victim of a name-caller? Call BERT!

Someone wore a Pocahontas costume to a Halloween party? Call BERT!

Snow penis on campus? Call BERT!

Yes, a snow penis. Yes, that did happen. Yes, the bias response team was called.

After a big snowstorm in Ann Arbor, someone built a giant penis out of snow outside a dorm at the University of Michigan. Someone there reported it as a bias incident. Wait, against whom exactly is the snow penis biased? Frostina the Snow Woman? Poorly endowed men? Ridiculous things like the snow penis were once simply known as college pranks, now it's bias. There's no sense of humor anymore. What a miserable existence to see bias and offense in everything, especially something as benign as sophomoric tomfoolery.

Of course, the offense is always tied to ideology. That's how Establishment thinking works. If a Christian found offense in someone's "devil" Halloween costume, would they be afforded comfort or derision? A heterosexual uneasy with someone's drag queen costume, do they find sympathy or mockery? Social justice is always one-sided.

Want to dress up as Joe the Plumber? Careful there, that represents the white oligarchy. Iron Man? He's patriotic *and* a man—a double dose of debasement right there. Dress up as Donald Trump? Awesome! Dress as Hillary? OMG, I'm offended!

Prejudiced attitudes on college campuses are rote. What's more concerning is the Establishment's mollycoddling mindset.

I'm not sure what message these universities are sending their students. If someone can't handle a Halloween costume, name-calling, a word, or a snow penis, how will they handle a workplace or the global expanse of real life?

The good news is, if a white guy is walking the campus dressed as Barack Obama, BERT is standing by! Maybe he can help you man up.

CHAPTER 6

PROFESSOR PROGRESSIVE, PHD

When a college professor calls for the execution of the sitting president of the United States or that another would suggest the president's supporters be beaten up, or when one calls for House Republicans to face a firing squad, and that these professors are still employed and not in jail, then our campuses are less institutions of higher learning than they are Establishment proving grounds raising up the next Pol Pot.

When a professor gives students a choice between protesting Donald Trump or writing a research paper, are they educating or indoctrinating?

Is there greater elitism than when a university offers an anti-Trump course?

This is higher education in Establishment America.

The gateway to greener pastures is just a swamp covered in hatred.

Take Lars Maischak. He's a lecturer at California State University, Fresno with a PhD from Johns Hopkins. For someone with credentials like that you'd think him more astute than to get on Twitter one day in early 2017 and call for a presidential lynching . . . "To save American democracy, Trump must hang. The sooner and the higher, the better. #TheResistance #DeathToFascism."

Eloquent? Not so much. Emissary of debate? Nah. Maischak also doesn't seem to know what "fascism" means relative to our constitutional republic or how the word accurately describes the way in which things were run by the last president America had *before* Donald Trump. What's worse, Maischak and his ilk are in classrooms across the country ~~indoctrinating~~ educating millions of young adults every single day. That should scare the hell out of you. After some bad press and a Secret Service inquiry, Maischak apologized for his comments, but truth be told, I haven't trusted anyone named "Lars" since Metallica destroyed Napster.

There was a time before angst and vitriol co-opted campus dialogue when professors were sages to wide-eyed neophytes. Many still are, but many esteem themselves above the rest of us—that's a basic tenet of the Establishment. And from this flawed yet pervasive mindset sprung histrionics disguised as civil discourse, subversion masked as dialogue, and hysterics branded as passion. How else to explain the utter and totally certifiable meltdown of a professor from New York University while protesting a campus talk given by conservative firebrand Gavin McInnes.

Does this professor encourage healthy debate? Not likely. She joined a mob of like-minded malcontents there to heckle McInnes. That's what these Establishment "educators" do in the new Trump reality. Screaming at the top of her lungs, the professor berated police officers, cajoling them to beat up

McInnes and his supporters, "You should kick their ass!" So, to this person, a person tasked with shaping young minds, it is a duty of the police to physically attack people with whom the Establishment disagrees. That's quite the lesson for her students.

Ever see the 1981 film *Scanners*? There's a scene in it where a guy's head literally explodes. Look up the YouTube clip of this McInnes incident at NYU and you'll see a professor so unglued, so full of unmitigated rage, she appears *thisclose* to her own head exploding, which, candidly, would be substantially more entertaining than *Scanners*.

As police officers worked to quell the mob and protect McInnes, the professor screamed at them, "You are f**king a**holes! This is a joke! You're protecting the Nazis! This is a f**king joke!" What delicious irony as the real joke came with this punch line, "You should be protecting these students from *hate!*"

Truly, nothing is funnier, in an ironic unemployed-hipster-complaining-about-capitalism-on-a-$700-iPhone kinda way, than a person with forehead veins popping, screaming until their voice is hoarse, using language so foul it's tough to believe they kiss their mother with that mouth, and so indignant their face is cherry red, calling *someone else* hateful. The only hate on that night came from the professor and her ~~minions~~ students.

They don't see their hypocrisy, or they do, but just don't care. Remember, the Establishment fancies itself smarter than the rest of us. Condescension is a cornerstone. The normal rules don't apply, at least not to them.

This is campus life post-Trump victory.

On the campus of the Art Institute of Washington just outside Washington, DC, you'll find Professor John Griffin. Shortly after the House of Representatives passed the American Health Care Act—the Obamacare replacement bill "deplorables" call Trumpcare—Professor Griffin shared a *Washington Post* editorial on his Facebook page. He showed true facility of speech when he wrote about Republicans representatives, "They should be lined up and shot. That's not hyperbole; blood is on their hand."

Sure, let's kill the lawmakers with whom we disagree. Wait, whose hand would the blood be on?

So, to be clear, murder is the path to good health care?

Thanks Professor, for clearing that up. I'll let you get back to reading *Mein Kampf*.

Over at Arizona State University, home of booze-fueled romps from Mill Avenue to Old Town Scottsdale and bleached blondes fancying themselves the next Giuliana Rancic as they unironically attend the Cronkite School of Journalism, you'll find a professor who gave her students a choice: hold a protest or write a research paper as a final assignment. In this environment of academic excellence, which choice do you think the students made?

So, on April 13, 2017, students of Dr. Angeles Maldonado, PhD, grabbed signs emblazoned with the slogan "Wall Against Hate" and took their places in front of Hayden Lawn on the ASU campus. Roughly two dozen students, all enrolled in Maldonado's "Global Politics of Human Rights" class, formed a human wall near the library, linking arms, and blocking people from passing.

Maldonado would later explain to the *Arizona Republic* how the protest originated in class discussions of President Trump's executive orders restricting travel from certain Muslim countries and his strong rhetoric on illegal immigration. What the good professor failed to mention was that her husband is an activist and immigration attorney who handles deportation defense cases and that in addition to her job at ASU, Dr. Maldonado *also* works in his law office. As I write this passage, Ray A. Ybarra Maldonado's Facebook profile picture is of him and his wife with the words, "I voted against Arpaio today" splashed on top in red, white, and blue. To say Professor Maldonado was without an activist agenda at ASU would be disingenuous at best.

Instilling in young adults the importance of debate, civil disobedience, the First Amendment, and fighting the status quo is a tremendously important responsibility. These are principles of freedom. Standing up for your beliefs and pushing against injustice is a cornerstone of American ideals. If our forefathers stood idly by while King George III forced all manner of oppression on them, where, as a country, would we be now? The issue at ASU is that a professor at a public university appears to have used her position with her students to further her own Establishment agenda.

Were any of Maldonado's students *supporters* of President Trump? Would they have felt safe enough to admit it? Would they have been ostracized? Free to disagree without reprisal? Attacked like Gavin McInnes at NYU? Given a failing grade? That anyone would be ashamed to admit they support the president illustrates just how morally bankrupt campuses have become.

It's one thing when it's the professors pushing one-sided thought, but when the universities themselves validate Establishment rhetoric, then we've reached an entirely new level of subversion.

Butler University, a private school in Indianapolis, now offers a course called "Trumpism and U.S. Democracy." Before a tsunami-sized backlash forced the school to change the course description, it claimed Donald Trump won the presidency by "perpetuating sexism, white supremacy, xenophobia, nationalism, nativism, and imperialism." They failed to mention that he orchestrated the breakup of the Beatles, was the second gunman on the grassy knoll, and didn't cry when Old Yeller got shot. It makes sense why the course would prepare students to, as outlined in the description, "discuss, and potentially engage in, strategies for resistance."

Strategies for resistance?

Are they teachers or activists?

With the Establishment, there's very little difference. Education means implanting a skewed worldview into impressionable minds. The sad thing is, the same students believing themselves intellectually astute can't name the current vice president. Nor can they find Nebraska on a map, much less Pakistan. They call Donald Trump a "xenophobe" but don't know the difference between xenophobia and patriotism. These young people are our future? Chew on that.

At Butler, needing to mitigate its public relations problem caused by the anti-Trump course, the school announced on its Facebook page that the faculty member (responsible for the course) had updated the course description, or more accurately, softened the toxic hyperbole: "Students will be looking at the rise of President Trump as a political and social phenomenon and are not required to participate in activism." Okay, so they're not *required* to participate in activism. Sure. Butler is basically Stan, the manager at Chotchkie's in *Office Space* who passive aggressively makes his employees wear buttons to show their "flair", but does it in such a way that it's not a "requirement," even though it really is. Activism is Butler's version of flair: "Look, we want you to express yourself, okay? Now if you feel that the bare minimum is enough, then okay. But some people choose to wear more and we encourage that, okay? You do want to express yourself, don't you?"

Activism isn't required but it is encouraged.

Any questions? Just ask Professor Progressive, PhD.

CHAPTER 7
"SORRY, GOD. YOU'RE EXPELLED."

The agenda of Western universities is to produce (left-wing) secularists. The difference is that Christian and Jewish seminaries are honest about their agenda, while the universities still claim they have neither a secularist nor a political agenda.

–Dennis Prager
Author, columnist, syndicated radio talk show host

God's been kicked out of college.

It's no wonder millennials espouse Establishment views. Morality, decency, and the recognition of something greater than ourselves don't exist on campus. Nihilism, narcissism, socialism, secularism—basically all the "isms"—waft through halls of education choked with the stench of dying principles.

The issue isn't just that religion, or more pointedly, Judeo-Christian values, are ignored or disrespected by Establishment professors, it's the deliberate full-scale offensive against those values *and* the people who hold them.

One day, Mark Holden, a twenty-two-year-old history major, showed up early to a class at Northern Arizona University in Flagstaff. He had some time before class started, so the self-described Christian opened his Bible and began to read. Holden's teacher, assistant professor Dr. Heather Martel, PhD, ordered Holden to put the Bible away.

Holden refused.

Martel summoned the department head, Derek Heng.

Heng told Holden to put the Bible away.

Martel later claimed the story "is a lie."

A lie?

Holden recorded the incident.

BAM!

Holden sent the audio to Kevin Cavanaugh, a Republican candidate for the House of Representatives in Arizona's First Congressional District, who forwarded it to the college watchdog group Campus Reform, which then posted the audio on its website and YouTube.

Heng: "So, Professor Martel says that she doesn't want you sitting in front of her because you put, you know, a Bible out. Right?"

Holden: "Uh-huh."

Heng then explains that his primary goal is to ensure the class goes on and that Holden is in it.

Holden: *"She doesn't want me in the front because I have my Bible out."*

Heng: *"No, I think she, I mean, well, why do you have your Bible out anyway?"*

Holden: *"I'm just reading it before class. Class hasn't even started yet. I'm reading my Bible."*

Heng: *"So, will you, will you, will you, put your Bible away?"*

Holden: *"I always do. Every day. And I read the Bible before class and I put it away before class starts."*

Had Holden been Muslim and reading the Quran, is there any question there'd have been zero conflict with the professor? I'll ask this again later, so keep reading. (How's that for a tease?)

This student, on his own time before class, quietly read a Bible and triggered a professor. Martel should have called BERT.

Should we be surprised there's misotheism in a classroom run by someone whose resume includes the works "Colonial Allure: Normal Homoeroticism and Sodomy in Sixteenth-Century French-Timucuan Encounters in Florida" and "Topics in Women's and Gender Studies—Global Queer History and Theory"?

On an institutional level, the blind hatred of Christianity is so pervasive at schools like NAU, they might as well be in Iran. Don't dare to bring out a Bible in public. The Establishment wears intolerance like a second skin.

A student like Holden has gumption. He spoke up. But how many conservative, Christian, or Jewish students don't have that? They fear reprisal. They fear a failing grade. They fear ostracism. For right-leaning professors, they fear unemployment.

Establishment institutions rule by fear.

At Rollins College in Winter Park, Florida, a suburb of Orlando, administrators suspended a Christian student after he challenged his Muslim professor's claim that Jesus' disciples doubted His divinity and that His crucifixion never happened.

In a class discussion and in a lengthy email, Marshall Poston pushed back against the anti-Christian contentions of a Muslim professor named Areej Zufari and learned the hard way how petty and vindictive an Establishment educator can be. Zufari, who, at the time, taught Middle Eastern Humanities, unceremoniously reported Poston to the college's dean of safety, claiming *she* felt unsafe. Well, of course. There's nothing more terrorizing than rhetoric and an opposing view.

The school administration claimed Poston was suspended for a social media post. If you buy that, I've got some alligator-free waterfront property on Lake Okeechobee I'd like to sell you.

What if, and I'm just spit-balling here, an Anglo professor asserted Muhammad was not a prophet of Allah and a Muslim student challenged the assertion? Would that student be reported and suspended? Who would Rollins College stand behind, the student or the professor?

You don't need a degree from Rollins College to know the answer.

Zufari later resigned from Rollins when the blowback from the ensuing media storm became too much to bear. Welcome to Karmatown! Population: Y-O-U.

•••

In 1992, the Library of Congress hosted an exhibition called "Revelations from the Russian Archives," which offered incredible insight into life behind the Iron Curtain. It's still accessible online. It's a fascinating read that could easily be mistaken for a modern American Establishment playbook, particularly a compelling passage titled "Anti-Religious Campaigns." It reads in part:

The Soviet Union was the first state to have as an ideological objective the elimination of religion. Toward that end, the Communist regime confiscated church property, ridiculed religion, harassed believers, and propagated atheism in the schools. Actions toward particular religions, however, were determined by State interests, and most organized religions were never outlawed.

Is there much difference between the Soviet Union and the administrations at many of today's American colleges?

•••

About forty minutes from downtown Atlanta, Georgia, nestled amongst the trees and lush landscape is the beautiful campus of Georgia Gwinnett College in Lawrenceville. But the beauty belies an ugliness of a demonstrably anti-Christian administration. How else to characterize an entity that describes the Gospel message of the Bible as "fighting words"?

In December of 2016, the Alliance Defending Freedom (ADF) sued GGC on behalf of a student named Chike Uzuegbunam. They claimed the school systematically prevented Uzuegbunam from talking about his Christian faith on campus, despite that he had secured permission to do so in the school's designated free-speech zones.

Hold up! Huh?

Designated free-speech zones?

Shouldn't the *entire* campus be a free-speech zone?

At GGC, less than 1 percent of the campus is designated a "free-speech zone"—0.0015 percent of 260 acres to be precise. There are two zones. Students must be approved to use them. They're not open on weekends. During the week, they're available for eighteen hours, not per day, but for the *entire week*.

At GGC, free speech is paramount, for eighteen whole hours a week.

Only in Establishment America does one leave behind Constitutionally guaranteed protections by enrolling in college.

Uzuegbunam followed all the rules and jumped through every one of the school's bureaucratic hoops. He sought and received authorization to use the free-speech zones. He stayed within the free-speech zones as he shared the Gospel with fellow students. But that's never good enough when the Establishment is in charge—not if there's an agenda to be followed.

The suppression of free speech, especially religious speech, bears all the markings of Heinrich Himmler, oppressive yet dapper, in a pressed and starched poly-blend uniform. You can almost hear GGC ~~Gestapo~~ security yelling, "*Halt! Freie Rede ist verboten!*"

Translation: Stop! Free speech is forbidden!

The school denies censoring Uzuegbunam. Its defense for shutting him up? Uzuegbunam's words rose to the level of "fighting words." You can't argue with that. If the Establishment has taught us anything it's that the most hostile word in the world is spelled G-O-D.

CHAPTER 8

EAT MOR CHIKIN

I could eat a Chick-fil-A sandwich every day of the week and twice on Sunday—if Chick-fil-A was open on Sunday. A Chick-fil-A chicken sandwich is 440 calories of hand-breaded, pressure-cooked, beautifully seasoned, boneless chicken breast sitting on a buttered bun of pure perfection. Add waffle fries and a sweet tea and you have a meal God likely serves in Heaven.

A Chick-fil-A sandwich is culinary craftsmanship. But on some college campuses, a Chick-fil-A sandwich is a messenger of doom hatched in the abyss as a symbol of non-inclusive terror the world over.

A chicken sandwich.

Shortly after Duquesne University in Pittsburgh, Pennsylvania, announced that its remodeled, on-campus food court would include Chick-fil-A Express, a ~~snowflake~~ student expressed fear that their safe place would be at risk.

Their safe place would be at risk? Because of Chick-fil-A?

See, these Establishment chickenphobes bought into a narrative that Chick-fil-A is an intolerant business discriminating against homosexuals.

That narrative is a lie.

In 2012, the CEO of Chick-fil-A, Dan Cathy, gave an interview to the *Biblical Recorder* newspaper, which was reposted by *Baptist Press*, where he articulated his *personal* view that as a Christian he supports "traditional" marriage. What the Establishment won't tell you is that as a company, Chick-fil-A takes no position whatsoever on the issue of gay marriage. (Note to Establishment contrarians: in 2008, in the final days before the presidential election, Barack Obama told MTV News, "I believe marriage is between a man and a woman. I am not in favor of gay marriage." Yet, you still voted for him.)

Once the Cathy interview gained traction, the Establishment seized the chance to brand Chick-fil-A as homophobic and to launch a nationwide boycott. It wasn't enough to destroy the man, they had to destroy his business too. They failed on both fronts. But in the Establishment mindset, any individual with a differing opinion must be obliterated.

The founder of Chick-fil-A, the late Truett Cathy, took homeless people into his home. His company's foundation, to this day, provides for affordable child care, education for working families, skill training for kids in disadvantaged neighborhoods, and free homework assistance throughout Atlanta, Georgia, where the company is headquartered.

Chick-fil-A is clearly evil.

Facts were lost on Establishment sycophants at Duquesne, at least with the school's Lambda Straight-Gay Alliance and a student senator named Niko Martini. He asked the school to reconsider bringing Chick-fil-A on campus because, as he told the university's newspaper, the *Duquesne Duke*, "Chick-fil-A has a questionable history on civil rights and human rights."

Oh, really? A questionable history on civil rights? Here's a question: Can anyone honestly say they've ever heard a cashier at any one of Chick-fil-A's 2,100 locations ask for someone's sexual orientation before taking their order? Can anyone honestly say they've ever seen a Chick-fil-A location deny service to a homosexual or a same-sex couple or a minority? Has Chick-fil-A ever announced homosexuals or minorities aren't welcome in their restaurants? Curiously, I *have* heard of Establishment-embracing workers at *other* fast-food chains denying service to police officers and the military. Does Martini, or any of his Establishment cronies, boycott those places?

When Duquesne announced the addition of Chick-fil-A to its food court, Scott Richards, the executive director of Duquesne's Auxiliary Services, proudly announced the news, "More than 245 college campuses around the country, including Catholic University, Penn State University, Drexel University, and the University of Pittsburgh, have successfully brought Chick-fil-A onto their campuses, and more are doing the same in the next several years. Now, our students will have the opportunity to enjoy the brand on our campus." So, it seems, institutionally, Duquesne had no qualm with Chick-fil-A. The only issue arose from coddled Establishment cowards in the student body who, to serve their own agenda, don't just buy into a lie, they propagate it. They demand safe spaces to protect themselves—but from what exactly? An opposing viewpoint? A waffle fry?

One of Duquesne's most notable alumni, retired US Army Ranger Sean Parnell, summed it up on Fox News' *Fox and Friends*:

They're a bunch of babies. College is supposed to prepare you for the real world, not shield you from opposing opinions, and safe spaces do exactly that. My message is: toughen up. There are no safe spaces in the real world. If you're going to be successful in this life after you leave college you've got to learn to embrace adversity and open yourself up to a litany of different opinions.

The intrinsic irony of this entire issue is that Duquesne is a *Catholic* university. In 2016, Pope Francis released his teachings on marriage and family in an "apostolic exhortation" called *The Joy of Love: On Love in the Family*. In this tome, the Pope reaffirmed the Church's position opposing same-sex marriages:

We need to acknowledge the great variety of family situations that can offer a certain stability, but de facto or same-sex unions may not simply be equated with marriage.

In discussing the dignity and mission of the family, the Synod Fathers observed that, "as for proposals to place unions between homosexual persons on the same level as marriage, there are absolutely no grounds for considering homosexual unions to be in any way similar or even remotely analogous to God's plan for marriage and family." It is unacceptable "that local Churches should be subjected to pressure in this matter."

The leader of the Catholic Church opposes same-sex unions; Duquesne is a Catholic school. To use the logic of the students opposing Chick-fil-A because its CEO opposes same-sex unions, given Pope Francis' position, shouldn't the students boycott Duquesne and, for that matter, Catholicism itself?

But there's nary logic in an Establishment view. Take this ~~idiot~~ professor at Eastern Illinois University, Dr. Lisa Moyer, PhD, who wanted EIU to oust Chick-fil-A from campus. In an interview with Campus Reform, Moyer said the restaurant was a symbol of hate and claimed Chick-fil-A "made a lot of students, particularly in the LGBT community, feel uncomfortable."

Dr. Moyer, if a fast-food joint with a sterling record for outstanding customer service and good works in the community makes you uncomfortable, let's get you a first-class airplane ticket to Syria. Perhaps you can secure a courtside seat for when the Islamic State executes a homosexual just for being homosexual. Then you can come back and tell us how hateful and oppressive Chick-fil-A is.

In fact, why don't you take a former student body president of the University of Nebraska Kearney with you?

In early 2016, a UNK decision to bring Chick-fil-A to campus was thwarted after a group of students complained about Dan Cathy's views on marriage. (Yawn.) The university's student body president at the time, Evan Calhoun, responded to those complaints with a Facebook post, since deleted, that was as ignorant as it was loquacious:

When we learned more about Chick-fil-A and its corporate values and discriminatory policies, and after hearing these concerns raised by a section of our student body, we concluded that these corporate values are not aligned with our values as a student body, and it is not in the best interest of our UNK community to pursue Chick-fil-A right now.

Discriminatory policies?

Name one.

I double-dog dare you.

Name a single Chick-fil-A corporate policy that's discriminatory. If you can find even one, I'll buy you a Chick-fil-A combo meal with extra honey mustard sauce. I'll even throw in an Icedream® cone and a cookie.

As for the corporate values that are "not aligned with our values as a student body," they include:

To glorify God by being a faithful steward of all that is entrusted to us and to have a positive influence on all who come into contact with Chick-fil-A.

Everyone's job at Chick-fil-A is to serve. No matter our title or job description, our reason for coming to work is to generously share our time and talents. Whether it's treating customers like friends, or serving our communities like neighbors, we believe kindness is a higher calling.

From donating surplus food to local shelters and soup kitchens through our Chick-fil-A Shared Table program, to feeding victims *and first responders after a disaster, our restaurant Operators give away food all year long to those who need it most.*

"These corporate values are not aligned with our values as a student body." Wow. That says a lot about the Duquesne student body as described by Calhoun. To find offense in decency and goodness is the ethos of the Establishment.

When Calhoun was elected student body president, he gave an interview posted on the UNK website, where he shared his main goal, which was "to strengthen the relationship between Student Government and different organizations around campus." Evan, between you and me, if you want to strengthen relationships with organizations, don't alienate them. UNK has eight campus ministry organizations. Don't you think some of the students involved in those organizations *agreed* with Cathy's position on traditional marriage?

No matter. A year later, UNK regents approved a renovation of the student union, which includes—you guessed it—Chick-fil-A.

The rigmarole of keeping Chick-fil-A off campus wasn't limited to Duquesne, Eastern Illinois, and Nebraska Kearney. Johns Hopkins, Fordham, and a few other schools, less notable, tried too.

Ultimately, what this issue boils down to is that Establishment sheep who inhabit college campuses hate free thought, free speech, opposing views, tolerance of ideas, inclusiveness, and apparently, awesome chicken sandwiches.

Thank God Kentucky Fried Chicken wasn't coming to any of these schools—the professors and students would really need a safe space. With Colonel Sanders being a white Southerner and all, surely, he must be a racist, deplorable, Trump supporter.

CHAPTER 9

DUDE, WHERE'S MY SAFE SPACE?

Safe spaces.

There's much ado about these celebrated cells of solace, sprung forth from college campuses coast to coast, rendering respites from the harshness of life (and alliteration) in Trump's America.

Fifty years ago, the only safe spaces in America were the ones people built under their homes to protect against a Soviet nuclear attack. Now, the Establishment creates them as a shield from the atrocities of—oh, the horror—different opinions!

Historically, a safe space was a place where students, usually gay, could gather and talk without fear of attack or insult. It was a place where one could find support, encouragement, and empathy. Now, they're nothing more than panic rooms for emotionally stunted echo boomers too weak to handle viewpoints that make them uncomfortable. They're the mollycoddled generation, unaware of how the world works, in search of a phantom Utopia where groupthink replaces individual thought and Shangri-La is like-mindedness, absolute.

Sorry kids, Stepford is not a real place.

It's the generation of participation trophies, where the pursuit of excellence has no payoff, and people like Bernie Sanders say life is unfair.

It's why Ohio State University offered a "safe space" for students during the inauguration of Donald Trump. Life is unfair. The election was unfair.

As is always the case with the Establishment though, fairness goes just one way. Did Ohio State offer a safe space when Barack Obama was inaugurated?

Safe spaces shield students from ideas and speech with which they don't agree. Outward hostility manifests as internal fear. A philosophical difference isn't just, well, a difference, it's a trigger.

The Establishment doesn't see the world in absolutes. For them, absolute is closed-minded. Absolute is intolerant. Absolute is nonprogressive.

In the Establishment's mind's eye, truth is fluid. There's your truth, and there's my truth.

Race is fluid. If you're white but feel black, then you are black.

Gender is fluid. If you're woman but identify as a man, then you are a man. If you're a man but identify as a woman, then you are a woman.

These are the norms within the Establishment. Embrace a counterview and woe to you. More precisely, woe to you if you are a straight, white male. Then, there *is* an absolute—you are absolutely the devil.

This type of thinking drives places like Duke University to dream up the Men's Project, a safe space designed for the "male-identified" to bash male privilege.

The male-identified? I believe you mean "men."

Curiously, the Men's Project was not created by men, it was created by the Duke Women's Center, because, of course it was. What real man would come up with a course whose primary aim, according to one of its leaders, Dipro Bhowmik, is to "critique and analyze their own masculinity and toxic masculinities"? No self-respecting man is sitting in a room with other self-respecting men figuring out ways to be less manly.

A real man should show up to one of these classes and yell, "Man up!" The word-police from Cal State Chico would suddenly appear and come down harder than a snow penis in Michigan.

The Men's Project describes itself as a place to "engage with conversations that are linked to masculinity and male privilege."

Male privilege? Does the Establishment ever weary of flogging that same dead horse?

Masculine men = Evil.

Masculine men = Toxic.

According to these wildebeests, masculinity exists under multiple spheres of oppression (like patriarchy, white supremacy, heterosexism, cissexism, and rape culture).

Shoot, I used the term "wildebeest." Clearly, I'm not just oppressive, I'm teeming with toxic masculinity too.

This is buffoonery rooted in identity politics and the victim mentality—two pillars of the Establishment.

America's roads are disintegrating. The infrastructure desperately needs an overhaul. Millions of people don't have a job. The national debt is colossal. Our southern border is more porous than a sieve. ISIS wants to kill us. But the real issues for Establishment simpletons are sexism, misogyny, racism, homophobia, transphobia, and, of course, whether men are too masculine.

Joe Six-Pack doesn't need a lecture, he needs a job. But screw him, says the Establishment. Joe has male privilege and masculinity.

●●●

In Arizona, ninety minutes from the Grand Canyon, moonbeams and unicorns fill the sky over Northern Arizona University—a campus of ethereal wonder, where safe spaces spring eternal, and hirsute sprites yield to slumber upon the last measure of "Kumbaya."

NAU—it's back—is the same wonderfully tolerant place, as you'll remember, where a professor stopped a student from reading the Bible before class. It's the same place where a professor docked a student's essay one point because, in the essay, the student used the word "mankind" rather than a word more "gender neutral." (Insert face palm here.) And NAU is the same place where students tried to get the university president fired for refusing to put safe spaces on campus.

You've heard the phrase, "The inmates are running the asylum"?

At a campus forum hosted by NAU's president, Rita Cheng, a ~~crybaby~~ sophomore named Breanna Kramer asked Cheng a question wonderfully multilayered in its degree of idiocy yet so altogether sublime as it illustrated the asinine mindset of today's Establishment college student:

How can you promote safe spaces if you don't take action in situations of injustice, such as, last week, when we had the preacher on campus and he was promoting hate speech against marginalized students?

Where to begin? First, there is no such thing as "hate" speech. Nothing in our Constitution or in any of our laws recognizes such a thing. "Hate speech" is no more than a nifty label given by Establishment dimwits to words they don't like and to verbally communicated ideologies with which they disagree. And surprise, surprise, surprise, it's *all* protected under the First Amendment.

Secondly—Kramer refers to having a preacher speaking on campus as an "injustice." Regardless of the content of his rhetoric, or whether you disagree with that rhetoric, it is not an injustice to allow a conflicting dogma a platform. It's the free exchange of ideas—an incredible benefit of a free nation and something for which people long before us fought and died. Kramer wanted NAU to "take action" against such a thing.

Third—Kramer wants the university to provide a "safe space." She, and others like her, feel entitled to this sort of currency. They're blissfully unaware the real world doesn't owe you a thing—certainly not a safe space.

The preacher to whom Kramer was referring was Brother Jed, a hellfire and damnation, fire-and-brimstone evangelist from an organization called the Campus Ministry USA. For the past thirty years or so, Brother Jed's been traveling to college campuses to teach, or more precisely, *scream* the Gospel. His words are particularly harsh toward homosexuals, and with his over-the-top, high-intensity delivery, Brother Jed's words can sound hateful, and he easily comes off looking like, quite frankly, a crazy person.

But what Kramer needs to learn is people like Brother Jed believe what they believe, just as Kramer believes what she believes. The First Amendment doesn't differentiate between the strength of someone's convictions, the loudness of their words, or the agreeability of their message. If you don't like what Brother Jed says, walk away. Simple as that. Screaming at him is a futile exercise. To anyone who has seen Brother Jed, it's painfully apparent there is no arguing with the guy. The worst thing you can do to a provocateur is to leave them speaking to an empty space.

Establishment students never learn.

Instead they seek safe spaces and at NAU, when they don't get one, they look to destroy their own university president.

The trigger for that was Cheng's response to Kramer's desire for a safe space:

As a university professor, I'm not sure I have any support at all for safe space. I think that you as a student have to develop the skills to be successful in this world and that we need to provide you with the opportunity for discourse and debate and dialogue and academic inquiry, and I'm not sure that that is correlated with the notion of safe space as I've seen that.

Bravo!

The university president believes students should develop the skills to cope in the real world *and* to embrace discourse and debate.

Of course, with such a common-sense position, outrage was sure to ensue. It always does when the Establishment has nothing to support their arguments. Students marched from the forum and demanded Cheng's resignation, and the NAU Student Action Coalition (SAC) organized a protest, which is pretty much all SAC does. Its Facebook timeline is an endless barrage of bitching. They're too ignorant to recognize that every time something upsets them, if all they do is stand on campus screaming, they're no different than Brother Jed.

The only thing a group like SAC accomplishes is to make them themselves believe they're making a difference.

They're not.

Still, in the face of theatrical petulance and childish temper tantrums, Cheng refused to back down. Instead, she reinforced her initial statement with a perfectly well-reasoned comment emailed to Phoenix television station KPNX:

NAU is safe. Creating segregated spaces for different groups on our campus only [leads] to misunderstanding, distrust and [reduces] the opportunity for discussion and engagement and education around diversity. Our classrooms and our campus is a place for engagement and respect—a place to learn from each other. NAU is committed to an atmosphere that is conducive to teaching and learning.

In a world where lunacy runs rampant across the landscape of academic administration, Cheng is niece Marilyn on *The Munsters*—the only normal one in a family of freaks.

Too bad students of the Establishment can't see how awesome an administrator like this is. But it's tough to see the outside world from within the walls of a safe space.

CHAPTER 10

THE NOTRE DAME WHINING IRISH

After seeing the debacle of its 2017 commencement, it's difficult to fathom the University of Notre Dame is the same school portrayed in *Rudy*, one of the all-time great inspirational films. As we know, it's the story of a student with a never-ceasing work ethic, extraordinary school pride, an aspiration for greatness that inspires others, and a constant drive to achieve a goal. Never does Rudy quit when life challenges him. Never do we see Rudy bad mouth an authority figure nor do anything to embarrass Notre Dame.

Fast-forward to 2017, when disgustingly ill-mannered, disrespectful juveniles—also known as some Notre Dame graduates—embarrassed themselves and the university by putting petulance, disrespect, and intolerance on display in front of the vice president of the United States.

Our lady of victory, pray for us, indeed.

Vice President Mike Pence was the principal speaker at Notre Dame's 172nd commencement, where he also received an honorary degree. A month prior, a couple of triggered seniors launched the #NotMyCommencementSpeaker campaign. And why not? Everyone knows the most lethal weapon against a perceived injustice is a hashtag. At least that's what it says on page 263 of *Establishment Whining for Dummies.*

One of the hashtag campaign organizers, Immane Mondane, told Notre Dame's student-run online newspaper, the *Observer:*

[Pence] represents the larger Trump administration . . . his administration represents something, and for many people on our campus, it makes them feel unsafe to have someone who openly is offensive but also demeaning of their humanity and of their life and of their identity.

It makes them feel *unsafe?*

Ideological differences?

Good luck on the outside, kids.

Jourdyhn Williams, the co-organizer of the anti-Pence campaign, felt the VP's appearance would violate Notre Dame's Catholic mission. "It goes against certain Catholic social teaching," she told the *Observer.*

Oh, really?

President Barack Obama delivered the commencement address at Notre Dame in 2009. A *pro-abortion* president speaking at a Catholic university? Did he go against "certain Catholic social teaching"?—like the Catholic social teaching of the United States Conference of Catholic Bishops:

The Catholic Church proclaims that human life is sacred and that the dignity of the human person is the foundation of a moral vision for society. This belief is the foundation of all the principles of our social teaching. In our society, human life is under direct attack from abortion and euthanasia.

Where was the Establishment's #NotMyCommencementSpeaker campaign then?

These crybaby students don't know their own school's history nor their own hypocrisy nor the tenets of the Catholic faith.

And they weren't the only ones.

A campus group called We Stand For, a coalition of Notre Dame student activists, launched its own hashtag campaign—#WalkOutND—and succeeded in getting what appeared to be a few dozen students, of the roughly 3,100 in attendance, to walk out of the stadium as Vice President Pence began speaking.

This group is made up of real geniuses. In its press release announcing the walkout, besides incorrectly dating it "2016" when the event took place in 2017, We Stand For declared its support for Notre Dame's LBGT+ community and, of course, the whole Catholic social teaching thing:

The participation and degree-conferring of VP Pence stand as an endorsement of policies and actions which directly contradict Catholic social teachings and values and target vulnerable members of the University's community.

It's always fun to see a group of Catholic university students chop up Catholic catechism like meat, selectively using the parts that serve their agenda and tossing the rest.

We Stand For believes the Trump administration is discriminatory toward the LBGT+ community—though there isn't a single shred of evidence supporting the contention—and, yes, *The Catechism of the Catholic Church* does preach the acceptance of homosexuals—to a degree:

The number of men and women who have deep-seated homosexual tendencies is not negligible. This inclination, which is objectively disordered, constitutes for most of them a trial. They must be accepted with respect, compassion, and sensitivity. Every sign of unjust discrimination in their regard should be avoided.

However, the catechism stating the acceptance of homosexuality is limited to the *person*—the homosexual individual—and not of homosexuality as a lifestyle, which the teaching undoubtedly forbids:

Basing itself on Sacred Scripture, which presents homosexual acts as acts of grave depravity, tradition has always declared that "homosexual acts are intrinsically disordered." They are contrary to the natural law. They close the sexual act to the gift of life. They do not proceed from a genuine affective and sexual complementarity. Under no circumstances can they be approved.

As for the transgendered—sorry dudes, chicks, or whatever you think you are—*The Catechism of the Catholic Church* demolishes the whole paradigm of self-identity:

Everyone, man and woman, should acknowledge and accept his sexual identity. Physical, moral, and spiritual difference and complementarity are oriented toward the goods of marriage and the flourishing of family life . . . By creating the human being man and woman, God gives personal dignity equally to the one and the other. Each of them, man and woman, should acknowledge and accept his sexual identity.

Given the position of Catholicism, and that Notre Dame is, after all, a Catholic university, and based on its argument for walking out on Vice President Pence, doesn't logic dictate We Stand For call for a boycott of Notre Dame itself? But then again, this is the same school that had its campus police silence traditional-marriage activists back in 2014. Nevertheless, with the Establishment, logic is never a driver of action.

The students who walked out on Vice President Pence?

Sheep.

Ignorant.

Rude.

Dumb.

Classless.

There's a difference between going to class and having class.

Did this self-aggrandizing truly accomplish anything, besides making themselves feel better?

Now that these students have graduated, hopefully they've found a safe space in the real world. If not, to be sure, they can always protect themselves with a vicious hashtag.

CHAPTER 11

ALL SIGNS POINT TO STRESS!

I was just thinking things over. I was, like,
meditating. Then I sort of watched myself
from inside. I realized it was ridiculous,
being afraid, worrying about everything.

–Cameron Frye
Ferris Bueller's Day Off

It's too bad students angling for safe spaces never seem to have the same catharsis as Cameron Frye–to recognize the ridiculousness of fearing the mundane.

In life, there are many stressful things: unemployment, divorce, financial problems, sickness, watching *The Bachelor*, and now–thanks to students at Harvard University–library fines.

Harvard, the crème de la crème of the Ivy League, the oldest university in the country and a bastion of northeastern Establishment elitism, has ended its fifty-cent per day fee on overdue library books. The reason is remarkably pedestrian and so perfectly "Establishment."

Steven Beardsley, Harvard's associate director for access services administrative operations—what a title—explained to the *Harvard Crimson* why the fines were dropped: "We have witnessed firsthand the stress that overdue fines can cause for students."

"The stress that overdue fines can cause for students."

Harvard—where future titans of industry, politics, science, and law grace its hallowed halls. Harvard—where presidents and senators learned the gravitas of excellence, character, and mettle. Harvard—where young adults are coddled because a fifty-cent library fine causes them stress.

How did one of the most prestigious universities in the world stoop to making such a rank and file decision?

To be fair, there was the time a Harvard librarian witnessed a student with a perfect amount of Philip B. pomade, wearing a Polo shirt, a cashmere Brooks Brothers sweater draped over his shoulders, and Outlier chinos telling his girlfriend, "I am so dreadfully sorry Bunny, I am unable to attend the debutante ball this evening. It is quite grievous, as you are delightfully coquettish. But you see, my dear, I was remiss in returning a book on mathematics to the repository in a timely fashion. Consequently, I am imbued with a very high level of stress. Please, pass along my sincerest apologies to Mumsie, Sir Alfred, and Master William. I shan't be available this night and I must now retire to my safe space. Good day."

What message is Harvard sending to its students? "Hey kids, if you borrow something and you're too irresponsible to return it on time, don't worry about it. There won't be any consequences! We know consequences stress you out."

Try this kind of Establishment logic in real life. Call your mortgage company and tell the representative the due date for your monthly payment has triggered an inordinate amount of tension. Surely, they'll eliminate your note altogether, because mortgage loan officers have seen firsthand the stress these loans can cause.

●●●

The administrators at Western Washington University apparently have yet to surmise the acute stress on students caused by a fifty-cent per day overdue book fine. How else to explain why their library still enforces one? One could presume the students at WWU are imbued with more emotional fortitude than their Harvard counterparts. But then you hear about a WWU student suffering an epic meltdown at the mere sight of a pro-Trump sign, and the presumption is blown to bits.

Less than four months after Donald Trump took the oath as president, a student was captured on camera, in video obtained by Campus Reform, throwing a spectacular conniption fit after seeing a street preacher holding a sign that said, "Trump: Borders, Laws, Jobs, Liberty, USA." To call what happened next a "meltdown" would be to grossly understate it.

For two solid minutes this ~~cupcake~~ student screamed uncontrollably. She threw things on the ground. She succumbed to the worst parts of "Trump Derangement Syndrome."

She had the stress level of a neurosurgeon with the pay scale of a video clerk. Maybe her name is Daria—the brainy, misanthrope student from the MTV series of the same name.

The entire episode would be nothing but a pathetic display of moronic behavior if not for the fact that it is emblematic of today's Establishment.

In all candor, a freak-out so over the top might very well have been a sort of performance art project. Regardless, it demonstrates the delicate psyche of young people on campuses today brought on by the relentless push of skewed ideas.

Truculent behavior is to be expected from indoctrinated students, but when a university itself loses it over a pro-Trump sign, then the problem isn't individual, it's institutional, and more deeply embedded than one may have realized.

At the University of South Alabama, a school official demanded a student remove a "Trump/Pence Make America Great Again! 2016" sign from the window of his dorm room—a ballsy move in a state where Trump destroyed Clinton by nearly thirty points. It's also an illegal move.

There's a document that appears not to have been read by the administrators at the University of South Alabama, it's called the *Constitution of the United States*—and to think the school's initials are U-S-A. Fortunately, the student who'd displayed the sign, David Meredith, did read the Constitution. When the school put the screws to him to take down the sign, instead of reacting as Establishment students do—by acting the fool—Meredith emailed a reply to the school. Two words: "First Amendment."

This is the beauty of a college student knowing their rights—political speech is always protected in the United States of America—and having both good sense *and* the intestinal boldness to push back against the Establishment.

Relatively speaking, it was an easy fight.

A community director who oversees the dorms emailed Meredith explaining that he "currently live[s] in a federal building that cannot support political candidates." How deliciously ignorant is this? Let us count the ways . . .

1) A dormitory at the University of South Alabama is not a *federal* building. It is a *state* building.

2) Given how Meredith put up his sign five months *after* the presidential election, Donald Trump and Mike Pence weren't *candidates*, they were the president and vice president.

3) If you accept the dorm is a federal building—which it is not, duh—you would have to ask the same thing Meredith did: "The name of the president and vice president cannot be posted on federal buildings?"

Check and mate.

The university dropped the whole thing.

You see, logic and truth are always a defense to ignorance—and much more effectual than demands for a safe space or claims of stress. Students like David Meredith make a difference. The battle isn't lost!

Never should a freedom-loving college kid cower from scalawags unable to manage life without a safe space. A flag-waving student guided by principle can't be defeated by a namby-pamby who finds stress in a library fine. And college patriots need not be strong-armed by bullies who hate America. Few things are more dangerous to the Establishment than conservatives who fight back—especially on campus.

CHAPTER 12

BERKELEY: WHERE FASCISM REIGNS AND FREE SPEECH GOES TO DIE

The word "fascist" is bandied about a lot in this current political climate. Along with "racist," it's the go-to word for the Establishment when they have no substance in an argument. From chapter 1 of *Establishment Arguing for Dummies*:

> When you don't have any facts to support your argument in a debate with a conservative, call them a "fascist." You can substitute "racist" for "fascist," and if the logic in your argument is really weak, use both. You needn't worry whether there's any evidence to uphold the accusation.

The patent absurdity of that tack becomes clear when the Establishment uses the forcible suppression of opposition to silence conservative views, which is a pillar of—*fascism!*

Without a hint of irony, they'll riot, incite violence, and stoke the suppression of opposing ideas oblivious to the reality that if there are fascists in this country, it's *them*.

No place in the United States is more ground zero for the Establishment's deliberate and forcible suppression of opposition than a college campus. And no campus is more illustrative of it than the University of California, Berkeley.

On the day of a scheduled speech, in February 2017, by Milo Yiannopoulos, a right-wing provocateur who, at the time, was an editor at *Breitbart*, violence exploded at Berkeley like a gas can filled with the incendiary hatred of contrary thought.

The Establishment reached new heights of hypocrisy.

A mob of hate-mongers screaming "fascist" launched firebombs, triggering campus police to put every building on lockdown. Berkeley rioters went full-on thug to shut down Yiannopoulos, so much so that cops sent a warning via Twitter to other students to get out for their own safety. A hundred grand in damages later, Berkeley cancelled Yiannopoulos' speaking engagement.

This is the devolution of what used to be the healthy exchange of ideas. The Establishment no longer even pretends universities are havens for free expression. It is clear—it openly hates all opposing ideologies and will not tolerate productive debate nor intelligent conversation.

The veil of pretense is lifted, and what's behind it is hideous.

Don't let Establishment pundits fool you—social justice warriors at places like Berkeley aren't wide-eyed students fighting for noble ideals. They're not protestors. They're terrorists. They use violence and coercion to push a political agenda, and *that* is straight-up terrorism.

A couple of months later, conservative author and columnist Ann Coulter accepted an invitation from the nonpartisan political organization BridgeUSA and Berkeley College Republicans to speak on immigration issues.

Pranav Jandhyala formed BridgeUSA following the Yiannopoulos fiasco with one primary goal. As he wrote in a special column for the *Washington Post*, it was "to facilitate dialogue between political opposites, allowing everyone to engage with and understand opposing viewpoints." He'd hoped to foster a culture shift to keep what happened with Yiannopoulos from ever happening again, and that Coulter's appearance at Berkeley would help facilitate it:

> *Coulter's ideas have an audience, and though most members of our group don't agree with her, we recognize the following she draws . . . But we believe the only productive way to fight views one sees as bad or dangerous is with better views . . .*

> *We planned for the event to be a debate-style Q&A with rebuttals to allow for a back-and-forth dialogue . . . Rather than repeating the failures of Yiannopoulos's event, we wanted to create a national example for what free discourse*

> *and the questioning of ideas should look*
> *like here at Berkeley, the home of the free*
> *speech movement 50 years ago.*

At Berkeley?

Good luck with that.

University administrators cancelled Coulter's appearance, citing threats of riots and violence. How deliciously pathetic. Students can't handle the expression of opposing ideologies so they riot to shut it down. This bunch needed an "empathy" tent on campus prior to an anti-Coulter demonstration to deal with it. No joke.

The admin folks who made the decision to cancel Coulter either lack intestinal fortitude, share the student's Establishment views—which is likely a 100 percent certainty, as former Obama lackey Janet Napolitano is the president of the University of California system—or they have no testicles—also a near 100 percent certainty.

Berkeley tried to get Coulter to speak on a different date—she refused. The date they'd chosen was at the end of the academic year when students were either long gone or taking final exams. The affront to free speech by the administrators and students at this citadel of intolerance was so naked, even the biggest Establishment mouthpieces turned on their own and defended Coulter's right to speak at Berkeley.

Former president Barack Obama at an A&E event in New York City: *Ann Coulter, at Berkeley, she should be allowed to speak. That's ridiculous, of course, she should be allowed to speak.*

Senator Bernie Sanders to *Huffington Post*: *Obviously, Ann Coulter's outrageous—to my mind, off the wall. But you know, people have a right to give their two cents-worth, give a speech, without fear of violence and intimidation.*

Television talk show host Bill Maher on *Real Time with Bill Maher*: *Berkeley used to be the cradle of free speech, and now it's just the cradle for f*cking babies.*

Maher even went so far as to criticize other college campuses for cancelling conservative speakers, saying, "I feel like this is the liberal version of book burning—and it's got to stop."

How can it stop? Not when we have people like the former head of the DNC, Howard Dean, out there, armed with a Twitter account and, not surprisingly, no understanding of the Constitution, spouting ignorant missives. Amid the Coulter controversy, Dean tweeted, "Hate speech is not protected by the First Amendment."

Again, with the "hate" speech thing?

To recap, for those raised in the Establishment: (A) There is no such thing as "hate" speech. And (B), if there were, yes, it would be protected by the First Amendment.

Perhaps they should retreat to an "empathy" tent to ponder this.

However, Berkeley administrators weren't the altruistic protectors of campus safety they'd have you believe. They too were complicit in shutting down conservative speech on campus. The university had six weeks notice of Coulter's appearance yet failed to plan for proper security measures surrounding the visit—then turned around and used security threats as the excuse for the cancellation. Afterward, according to a lawsuit filed in the wake of the cancellation, Berkeley attempted to move the location of the event several times and invoked an unwritten "high-profile speaker policy" that favors Establishment speakers and quashes conservative ones.

The lawsuit was brought by Berkeley College Republicans (BCR) and Young America's Foundation (YAF) against Berkeley's administrators, three Berkeley campus cops, and Janet Napolitano.

It alleges:

> *Though UC Berkeley promises its students an environment that promotes free debate and the free exchange of ideas, it had breached this promise through the repressive actions of University administrators and campus police, who have systematically and intentionally suppressed constitutionally-protected expression by Plaintiffs (and the many UC Berkeley students whose political viewpoints align with Plaintiffs), simply because that expression may anger or*

offend students, UC Berkeley administrators, and/or community members who do not share Plaintiffs' viewpoints.

Defendants engage in a pattern and practice of enforcing a recently adopted, unwritten and unpublished policy that vests in University officials the unfettered discretion to unreasonably restrict the time, place, and manner of any campus event involving "high-profile speakers"—a term that is wholly undefined, and that has enabled Defendants to apply this policy in a discriminatory fashion, resulting in the marginalization of the expression of conservative viewpoints on campus by any notable conservative speaker.

Defendants freely admit that they have permitted the demands of a faceless, rabid, off-campus mob to dictate what speech is permitted at the center of campus during prime time, and which speech may be marginalized, burdened, and regulated out of its very existence by this unlawful heckler's veto.

Those are damning allegations against the so-called "birthplace of the Free Speech Movement," where the intolerance of diversity of thought leads to the murder of free speech.

What's worse are the administrators who enabled it. They stood idly by while miscreants burned down the campus over Yiannopoulos—there was no measured distribution of consequence—then were duplicitous by acting the accommodating host to Coulter knowing full well they had no intention of allowing her to speak.

It's a pathetic testament to Berkeley and the subversive, unhinged antics of its ~~thugs~~ students—people too blinded by their hatred of America's stalwart freedom of speech to see the elemental irony of calling themselves "anti-fascists" while using violence to silence others.

SECTION 4

HOORAY FOR HOLLYWOOD!

CHAPTER 13

THAT SCREWY, BALLYHOOEY (HYPOCRITICAL) HOLLYWOOD!

Only in Hollywood does earning a living by playing make-believe elevate someone to dictate political discourse.

Only in Hollywood does possessing the talent to sing qualify someone as a policy wonk—foreign *and* domestic.

Hollywood, where naked avarice and unbridled narcissism are part and parcel, and a celebrity's love of self is matched only by self-importance and hypocrisy.

Hooray for Hollywood!

America's entertainment complex—an Establishment stalwart—so chockful of hubris masking a certifiably moronic mindset, it's home to the inanest of statements.

For instance, got a terrorism problem? Call Katy Perry. She'll solve it. The pop star/foreign policy and defense expert knows more than the Department of Defense and the State Department combined.

Need proof?

The day after an ISIS suicide bomber killed twenty-two people at a concert in Manchester, England, in May 2017, Perry went on the nationally syndicated radio program *Elvis Duran and the Morning Show* and laid bare the truth of eradicating terrorism: "I think that the greatest thing we can do is just unite and love on each other. No barriers, no borders, we all just need to coexist."

The bumper sticker on the barista's Subaru was right all along!

The solution to terrorism? Open the borders. Grab a jihadist and hug it out.

If only someone had loved on Omar Mateen, those forty-nine people he slaughtered at Pulse nightclub in Orlando would still be alive.

Perry's radio interview sounded absolutely idiotic. She doesn't grasp what's so funny about peace, love, and understanding is that none of it stops terrorists.

You cannot coexist with people who are trying to kill you.

Perry is so obtuse she didn't realize (or didn't care) that while calling for more unicorns and rainbows, she simultaneously blamed the victims. If only they had been more loving and kind and welcoming, then the bad terrorist person wouldn't have blown them up with a nail bomb.

If Perry is so enamored by love, coexistence, and barrier-free living, then why hasn't she invited Muslim refugees to live with her? Why hasn't she had a concert tour in Syria? Why, if I go to a Katy Perry gig, does a security guard tell me to empty my pockets, then subject me to a search with a handheld metal detector? Where's the love? Why is there a wall around Perry's $18 million home? I thought she didn't believe in barriers.

Perry is just another Establishment hypocrite in Hollywood, where the unspoken mantra is, "Do as I say, not as I do."

By the way, Katy, this "Resistance" movement you're in— Who are you? John Connor? Are you leading a makeshift militia in the quest to eliminate terminators and eradicate Skynet?

Girl, grab some cherry ChapStick, kiss a girl, make 'em go oh, oh, oh, as you shoot across the sky-y-y, and leave the diplomatic strategy to the professionals.

•••

Establishment hypocrisy runs the gamut in Hollywood. Filmmaker Michael Moore has a reported net worth of $50 million yet lambasts the very capitalism that made him all that money. Actor Mark Ruffalo marches with a crowd hatefully chanting "F**k Trump" while holding signs emblazoned "Love Trumps Hate." Even Piers Morgan—no friend to conservatives—saw it for what it was and tweeted, "Bomb threats, Hitler and incest taunts, foul-mouthed rants . . . and this was a march to 'End the hate'? Shameful hypocrisy." Barbara Streisand fights to keep people off her beachfront property but criticizes President Trump for wanting to build a border wall. The only thing bigger than Leonardo DiCaprio's hypocrisy is his carbon footprint—the one created by private jets and multiple homes.

Celebrities enjoy telling *you* how to live without the encumbrance of living that way themselves. They're above the mundane of the bourgeois. It's an Establishment trademark.

Hollywood lauds Roman Polanski, a degenerate child rapist who victimized a thirteen-year-old girl and who cowardly split for France to avoid facing the consequences—but assails then-candidate Trump for using inappropriate locker-room talk captured by an *Access Hollywood* microphone. They'll coronate Hillary even though her husband, whom they adore as the second coming of JFK, fancied himself some sort of *Shampoo*-era Warren Beatty as he groped and pawed his way from Arkansas to the White House. Establishment Hollywood defends rapists and sexual assaulters if they're politically aligned and, in Woody Allen's case, defends a guy accused of molestation who married his own stepdaughter— but they contend Mike Pence is hurtful to women because he won't eat alone with a woman other than his wife.

Establishment "logic" is so nonsensical it borders on *Onion*-like parody.

Amy Schumer promotes promiscuity on stage and on screen, makes the most vile, repellent jokes about female genitalia, yet takes part in the Women's March on Washington, DC, to stand up for the "rights" of women. Schumer must be unaware that women in America have the exact same rights as men. Can she, or anyone, name a single "right" men have that women don't? Second, has she, or any of those "pro-women" celebrities, marched against Islam? You know, the religion where the Quran says women are worth less men. Where were they when Bill Maher called Sarah Palin a "dumb twat" and a "c*nt"?

Oh, but in the Establishment, degrading, sexist insults are okay when the target is someone from the opposite side of the aisle—someone like, say, Ann Coulter.

During *The Comedy Central Roast of Rob Lowe*, panelist after panelist unleashed the word "c*nt" nineteen times at Coulter—one of their fellow "roasters" on the dais. No abbreviation. No "the 'C' word." They used the full word, in all its glory.

Nineteen times.

Sure, a roast, by nature, is void of decency and decorum. That's what makes them fun. It's good-natured teasing, at least it was when Dean Martin held them. But there's good-natured teasing and then there's disgusting, mean-spirited diatribe tossed around by witless Establishment hacks too tired, lazy, or morally corrupt to come up with a more intelligent insult.

Truth be told, Coulter *is* a provoker and a genius at guerrilla marketing her books, and often, the ire she attracts, she invites.

Nevertheless, that shouldn't matter. No woman, regardless of whether she tries to prove she is one, should ever be called a "c*nt."

It's not funny. It's not whimsical. It's not comedy.

It's sexist, vile, and dare I say, offensive.

There are a million ways to levy an insult at Ann Coulter. God knows she provides enough material. Her head was so far up Donald Trump's rear during the 2016 campaign, when he pooped, he thought it was a six-foot Cheeto until he realized, "Oh, never mind, it's just Ann." Look at that, an Ann Coulter insult without the "C" word. Imagine if actual, talented comedians made the effort on Comedy Central.

But this never was about comedy. It was about political ideologists, and not very bright ones, using the dais as a platform for partisan hate.

Can you imagine the widespread vitriol had it been say, Rachel Maddow targeted as a "c*nt" on that panel? The condemnation of the offending parties would have spewed like a sonic gusher of intolerance. But if the object for insult stands on the other side of the political spectrum, game on!

To Coulter's credit, she rebuffed the embrace of the victim mentality, subscribing to the oft-cited mom credo, "Sticks and stones may break your bones, but names will never hurt you." But just because she's tough enough to reject offense doesn't make a shameful display of hatred and vulgarity in the form of a repugnant word okay.

This assuredly won't be the last time we see this sort of thing from humorless Establishment hacks. But it's cool. A new political climate envelopes America, where silent deplorables are no longer silent and the more offensive the Establishment gets, the more evident it is patriots are winning, and where there's a new campaign slogan with an Election Day message for Hollywood hypocrites:

"See you next Tuesday!"

•••

Has a single Establishment celebrity complimented Kellyanne Conway? One would think a group of people so interested in the celebration of women would applaud the first woman ever to lead a winning presidential campaign in the United States of America. But in hypocritical Hollywood, the recognition of a woman's achievement is tied directly to whether they agree with your politics. So instead of celebration, Conway gets derision. How else to explain a ~~bitter Establishment shrew~~ television host, like the painfully unfunny Samantha Bee—who after nearly two lackluster decades in front of the camera finally ended up with her own show, *Full Frontal with Samantha Bee*—ripping Conway in a foul-mouthed rant? On her show the week of Trump's inauguration, Bee proved she's nothing more than an intolerant Hollywood hypocrite pushing the same boring talking points:

Kellyanne is the soulless, Machiavellian despot America deserves, not this undisciplined, hobbit-handed omni-shambles. Lean in, bitch. You're the one with superpowers. You changed history and also possibly ended it. So welcome to the hall of fame. If you'd like to pick up your award, it'll be behind our studio in the alley where women will be getting their abortions a year from now. Thanks for everything.

Only in the ramblings of an ignorant, tone-deaf elitist is the first woman nominated for president by a major party, but who ultimately lost, to be celebrated, while the first woman to lead the campaign that *won* be reviled.

•••

Lena Dunham talks about female empowerment. Does empowerment include falsely accusing an innocent man of rape, as she did in her autobiography?

Madonna calls for peace. She's compared herself to Martin Luther King but tells the crowd at the Women's March she's thought a lot about blowing up the White House. While it is true MLK had a dream, there is no evidence it included murdering the president with explosives.

James Franco laments the Trump presidency from a lap of luxury most people won't ever know, telling the *Daily Beast*, "I've spiraled into a depression and I've been questioning everything that I am, and how I've been doing things." The man has an Academy Award nomination, is an academic genius, and has a net worth of a reported $22 million. Sell your two-bit, hypocritical faux dramatics somewhere else, we're all stocked up here.

The Establishment applauded when Snoop Dogg "assassinated" President Trump with a gag gun in the music video "Lavender." The president failed to find the humor in the video but did note the hypocrisy, and tweeted:

Can you imagine what the outcry would be if @SnoopDogg, failing career and all, had aimed and fired the gun at President Obama? Jail time!

Exactly, but go one further. Try to imagine a Ted Nugent video in which the conservative rock star shoots Barack Obama in the head with a gag gun. What would the

Establishment do? Would they find it funny? Creative? In good fun?

We already know the answer to what they would do, because they already did it.

In 2012, Nugent made comments at a National Rifle Association convention in support of Mitt Romney's bid for president:

We need to ride into that battlefield and chop their heads off in November. If Barack Obama becomes the next president in November, again, I will either be dead or in jail by this time next year.

What happened? The Establishment exploded with outrage and Nugent got a visit from the Secret Service.

As Nugent later explained on Fox News' *The Specialists*:

My quote was that I was afraid if Obama was elected again I would either be dead or in jail because of all of the farmers and ranchers and citizens across this country who unload on me on a regular basis where they're being persecuted by various bureaucrats . . . I expressed fear of my government, But Pelosi and Feinstein and Boxer sent the Secret Service to investigate me and they concluded absolutely conclusively, I did not threaten anybody's life.

The hypocrisy is so disturbingly bare and so is their point—violence is okay when the object of the violence is conservative.

Hooray for Hollywood!

CHAPTER 14

"AND THE AWARD GOES TO . . ."

Award season is that glorious time between November and February when the Hollywood self-absorbed, wait, that's redundant—ahem—when Hollywood fellates itself, brags about gowns that cost more than the average person makes in a year, and spews disconnected rhetoric aimed at showing their fellow elites just how smart and socially conscious they are. At the same time, it proves to the rest of us just how smug, autocratic, and out of touch they really are.

Donald Trump is elected president and as sure as death and taxes, there's intolerance, hate, and bullying. No, not from him but from the Hollywood Establishment standing on awards show stages.

At 2016's American Music Awards, we bore witness to displays of arrogance so juvenile it often resembled a ninth-grade talent show, but not nearly as entertaining nor as intelligent.

One of the hosts, model Gigi Hadid, with the intellect one would expect from someone whose sole job is to stand and look pretty, began the night's proceedings with an excruciatingly bad "impersonation" of our First Lady, Melania Trump. The twenty-one-year-old Hadid squinted her eyes and with a poorly mimicked Slovenian accent said, "I love my husband, President Barack Obama. And our children Sasha and Malia."

The content of the "joke"—we get it. The controversy over whether parts of Melania's speech at the Republican National Convention were lifted from a speech given by former First Lady Michelle Obama—that's fair game. But the rest? Not so much.

Mocking an immigrant's accent? How progressive. How hilarious coming from a woman too dimwitted to recognize that her own father, Mohamed Hadid, is an immigrant with a thick accent. Imagine if a conservative mocked him, or for that matter, Michelle Obama? In fact, in eight years of awards shows during the Obama presidency, did any host ever ridicule the Obamas?

Hypocrisy thy name is Gigi.

Mean-spirited jokes at Trump's expense don't win votes to your side, so keep it up.

How about the American idiots known as Green Day? The long-in-the-tooth-trying-to-stay-relevant pop-punk band performed their song "Bang Bang," but changed some of the song's lyrics and chanted, "No Trump! No KKK! No fascist USA!"

So edgy! Nothing says punk rock more than shouting a maxim shared by everyone in the room. Remember when the essence of punk rock was having the guts to rail *against* what's popular? Punk rock takes backbone. Green Day had none. Had the band chanted, "Trump! Makes! America! Great!" *that* would have been edgy. That would have been so punk rock. I'm sorry, guys, but preaching to a choir? A punk band without testicular fortitude is nothing but noise.

As usual, no one in the room seemed to know the meaning of fascism. And, since when does strengthening border security equate to the Ku Klux Klan?

Celebrities cannot grasp the fact their candidate lost. These spoiled few, who are nary denied anything, are simply incapable of dealing with being told, "No." They throw tantrums. They're so tucked away in the safety of their Establishment bubble, they don't realize every time an awards show brims with anti-Trump commentary, the only thing accomplished is the alienation of half the country. The one substantive thing these elitists fail to embrace is the people who voted for Trump—people they brand as racist rednecks—also buy movie and concert tickets.

To insult them, well, that's just bad business.

But Hollywood never lets up.

The MTV Movie & TV Awards trotted out thirteen-term Democratic congresswoman Maxine Waters to present the award for "Best Fight Against the System." Waters herself is an award winner—"One of the Most Corrupt Members of Congress"—an honor she's received *five* times from Citizens for Responsibility and Ethics in Washington.

The Hollywood Establishment gave Waters a standing ovation when she walked onto the stage. That says everything you need to know about them.

These awards shows are pretentious displays of ignorance and intolerance and just so utterly predictable.

Was anyone surprised when Meryl Streep bashed Donald Trump after accepting her Cecil B. DeMille Award at the Golden Globes in 2017? Certainly, she believed it her moral responsibility as an esteemed member of the Hollywood Establishment. There's no point in being simply gracious when there's a worldwide platform available for resentful disparagement.

Streep pushed the false narrative that Donald Trump, when he was a candidate, mocked a disabled reporter at a campaign rally in South Carolina:

There was one performance this year that stunned me. It sank its hooks in my heart. Not because it was good. It was that moment when the person asking to sit in the most respected seat in our country imitated a disabled reporter.

That Trump mocked a disable reporter, Serge Kovaleski of the *New York Times*, was, of course, an Establishment lie fueled by a complicit media. It was reinforced by Hollywood's willing demagogues—like Streep.

To appreciate Streep's unflinching ignorance, one must know the genesis of this sad, sordid tale—comments Trump made at a 2015 campaign event in Birmingham, Alabama, and repeated in an interview on ABC's *This Week with George Stephanopoulos*, in which he claimed that on 9/11, people in New Jersey were cheering when the Twin Towers of the World Trade Center fell:

There were people that were cheering on the other side of New Jersey, where you have large Arab populations. They were cheering as the World Trade Center came down. I know it might be not politically correct for you to talk about it, but there were people cheering as that building came down—as those buildings came down. And that tells you something. It was well covered at the time, George. Now, I know they don't like to talk about it, but it was well covered at the time.

The establishment media, as it does, torched Trump for those comments. Trump, as he does, unearthed a 2001 newspaper story in the *Washington Post* that appeared to prove his assertion:

In Jersey City, within hours of two jetliners' plowing into the World Trade Center, law enforcement authorities detained and questioned a number of people who were allegedly seen celebrating the attacks and holding tailgate-style parties on rooftops while they watched the devastation on the other side of the river.

The writer of the story? Serge Kovaleski.

He wrote it when he worked for the *Washington Post.* Once the proverbial crap hit the fan following the Trump comments, Kovaleski conveniently denied remembering the details of his story—once it was evident that by doing so, he'd be helping Trump.

Fast-forward to a 2016 campaign rally in South Carolina. Trump mocked Kovaleski's backpedaling by acting discombobulated, with flailing arms, and uttering with halting speech, "Uh, I don't know what I said! Uh, I don't rememberrrr!"

Because Kovaleski is afflicted with arthrogryposis, a condition where some joints in the body have critically limited movement or are stuck in one position, the Establishment media quickly accused Trump of mocking his disability and broadcast an edited sound bite. To those who didn't know the whole story, that little nugget looked bad—very bad, indeed. But the media didn't tell its viewers the whole story, nor did it air Trump's *entire* speech—if it had, they'd have seen Trump later mock a general in the same way he did Kovaleski. It's Trump's go-to impression—like the time he mimicked Ted Cruz by acting discombobulated, with flailing arms, and halting speech—once again, like he did Kovaleski. There's video on YouTube of these rallies, first posted by a group called Catholics 4 Trump, where it's as plain as that smug grin on Meryl Streep's face, Trump isn't mocking a disability.

Is the "flustered arm-waving guy" impression, sophomoric? You bet it is. But it's a far cry from the sinister act the Establishment claims it to be.

The bigger question: Why is something like that even being talked about at a Hollywood awards show?

Answer: The Hollywood Establishment doesn't truly understand America. It lives in a biosphere so far removed from average, everyday Americans it simply cannot relate. What's worse—the celebrities think they're relatable. When self-worth is measured by what car looks best at the valet stand, there's not a lot of relating with real people happening there.

But there they are—superstars standing in front of millions of people—preaching to them.

At the 89th Academy Awards in 2017, Mexican actor Gael García Bernal condemned President Trump's plan to build a wall: "As a Mexican, as a Latin American, as a migrant worker, as a human being, I am against any form of wall that wants to separate us." Easy for you to say, hombre. Your birth country isn't the one under siege by people illegally sneaking into it. Your country isn't the one being fiscally sucked dry to the tune of $113 billion a year—that's billion with a "b" per year—at the expense of its own citizens.

Maybe García should stick to reciting lines someone else writes for him. Bueno?

Then there's Iranian director Asghar Farhadi. He won the Academy Award for "Best Foreign Picture." But like the petulant Establishment lackey that he is, Farhadi stayed home as a protest of the president's temporary travel ban on seven Muslim-majority countries, including Farhadi's. When he won, a statement Farhadi had written was read on his behalf:

My absence is out of respect for the people of my country and those of the other six nations whom have been disrespected by the inhumane law that bans entry of immigrants to the U.S. Dividing the world into the "us" and "our enemies" categories creates fear—a deceitful justification for aggression and war.

Another Hollywood Establishment minion spewing another false narrative. Farhadi is either ignorant of the truth or apathetic to it. The president's executive order didn't "ban entry of immigrants to the U.S." as Farhadi stated—it put a temporary moratorium on visas from those countries until visa applicants could be properly vetted. He also referred to the executive order as "inhumane." That's interesting coming from a man whose own country, Iran, amputates the limbs of people caught stealing, executes homosexuals, adulterers, and drug offenders, uses electric shock to "cure" children of homosexuality, flogs people for protesting, and imprisons people for Facebook posts—but Donald Trump is the inhumane one?

How can Farhadi ever be taken seriously?

Instead of spending time writing an awards show missive insulting the leader of the freest country on Earth, perhaps Farhadi should have complained to the leaders of his own country about *their* inhumanity? Yeah, that's right, he couldn't because they would have killed him! Filmmaker know-it-alls never see the irony.

You know who does? Real Americans.

The ratings for the Oscars telecast was its lowest in nearly a decade. Some industry professionals cited the expectation of anti-Trump commentary as some of the reason why people tuned out. Of course they tuned out! Real Americans are sick of it! Real Americans are sick of disengaged-from-reality pompous jerks insulting them. And the proof is in the numbers.

The cities with the highest number of viewers for the Oscars in 2017 were New York, San Diego, Los Angeles,

Chicago, and San Francisco. Hillary Clinton won every one of those cities in the 2016 presidential election. The cities with the lowest number of viewers? Memphis, Dayton, Winston-Salem, and New Orleans. Every one of those were carried by Donald Trump.

See a pattern?

Trump voters don't care if you live in a gated compound off Mulholland. They don't care if you fly private. They don't care about your pool. They don't care how many Twitter followers you have. They don't care about your latest box office receipts. And they certainly don't care about your opinion as to what's best for them and their families. They're not going to watch you belittle them and their choices.

But keep doing what you're doing at these awards shows, Establishment Hollywood, because the more you do, the longer Donald Trump and the anti-Establishment stays around.

CHAPTER 15

(NOT SO) FUNNY GIRLS

One of the truly great things about comedy is it often offers a welcome respite from the harsh realities of life. But when comedians swap comedy for those harsh realities of life, they're no longer comedians—*they're* the harsh realities from which we need an escape.

Does anyone go to a live comedy show or tune into a comedy television program to see a comedian spew rage and hatred instead of jokes? If I want to watch a preacher filled with indignation, I'll head over to Flagstaff the next time Brother Jed's at NAU.

Ever since the election of Donald Trump as president, "Trump Derangement Syndrome" has swept across the Establishment entertainment landscape like a plague afflicting scores of comedians, actors, and musicians. Symptoms include: fits of rage, violent tendencies, loss of logic, erratic behavior, megalomaniacal thoughts, incoherent rambling, sudden loss of reason, poor decision making, and feelings of superiority.

The afflicted will do odd and oft-offensive things, because they just can't help themselves. For instance, has-been actress, television host, and comedienne—if she can even be called a comedienne, given so few people find her funny—Kathy Griffin. The Z-list, anti-Trump "celebrity" teamed up with photographer Tyler Shields for one of the vilest displays of tastelessness and disrespect ever levied at a sitting president. In a grotesque photograph she posted on Twitter, Griffin stands in an ISIS-style pose, holding up President Trump's bloody, decapitated head, which she captioned, "I caption this 'there was blood coming out his eyes, blood coming out if his . . . wherever.'" (For the "antifas" at Berkeley, sorry, it was just a mockup and not Donald Trump's actual head.) Evidently, Griffin thought it clever to reference a nearly two-year-old comment candidate Trump made about then-Fox News anchor Megyn Kelly for asking him tough questions during a debate.

Griffin held up a bloody, severed head in the likeness of the president, but conservatives are the violent ones?

In the inevitable backlash—a virtual social media sh*tstorm—Griffin was flogged by people from all political persuasions: Chelsea Clinton, Keith Olbermann, Anderson Cooper, conservatives, liberals, Colonel Mustard with a candlestick in the library, and of course, President Trump and First Lady Melania.

So, as you do in these situations, Griffin posted a video in which she apologized:

> I'm a comic. I cross the line. I move the line, then
> I cross it. I went way too far. The image is too

disturbing. I understand how it offends people. It wasn't funny. I get it. I beg for your forgiveness. I went too far. I made a mistake and I was wrong.

Blah. Blah. Blah.

Griffin knew exactly what she was doing. In a behind-the-scenes video of the photo shoot, she was high-fiving the photographer as they looked at the picture. Then Griffin says to him, "Let's go to Mexico today because we're not surviving this." This was *before* she posted the ridiculous photo. Griffin knew the stir it would cause, and that's precisely why she posted it. Her "apology" was disingenuous at best.

With Griffin, orchestrated events like this are as much about political rancor as they are a desperate cry for relevancy. Like so many in the Hollywood Establishment, she confuses notoriety with relevance. But, God bless her, Griffin did achieve her goal—for a few news cycles, she was relevant. And luckily for her, no matter how moronic the effort to be "shocking," it's protected by the Constitution.

But Griffin learned an expensive lesson: the First Amendment doesn't guarantee freedom from consequences. She lost her commercial deal with Squatty Potty—vaguely ironic given her material is mostly crap—was fired from her job hosting CNN's New Year's Eve special, had the remainder of her comedy tour performances cancelled, and got a visit from the Secret Service.

Of course, an Establishmentarian always plays the victim. A couple of days after posting her "apology," Griffin held a news conference with her attorney, Lisa Bloom—who chases publicity like a late-night TV commercial lawyer chases ambulances—where *she* claimed to be the victim of Donald Trump. As conservative commentator Dana Loesch tweeted at the time, "It was almost as if HE took a photo with her severed head and not the other way around."

With an acting performance that was almost on par with a junior high school drama student, Griffin broke down in tears and through halting sobs accused the First Family of mobilizing "their armies" against her. "I'm going to be honest. He broke me. He broke me. He broke me." Griffin put the blame on President Trump for the loss of her various gigs.

Blaming others for *her* actions? Who does Griffin think she is? Hillary Clinton?

The news conference was absurdist theater at its finest, with a packed room, crocodile tears, and Griffin doing her best impression of Norma Desmond in *Sunset Boulevard* by overacting as though her life depended on it. Griffin played the victim card, the misogyny card—"It's a bunch of white guys trying to silence me. This wouldn't be happening to a guy"—*and* the sexism card, telling the gaggle of reporters if she was a man, the Secret Service would never have investigated her.

Tell that to Ted Nugent.

One can only wonder whether Griffin believes her performance art, or whatever she considered it, was worth the cost just to get attention. She lost gigs, achieved the rare feat of getting both liberals and conservatives to be pissed off at the same time, and raised the ire of the most powerful man in the world. Griffin hadn't screwed up that bad since telling Anderson Cooper on live television she was going to tickle his sack.

What's particularly sad is Griffin didn't care that President Trump has children; his youngest but eleven years old. It didn't matter that Barron might see it—and according to this tweet from the president, Barron did:

Kathy Griffin should be ashamed of herself. My children, especially my 11 year old son, Barron, are having a hard time with this. Sick!

Of course, Bloom questioned the truth of the president's comment, which is emblematic of the Establishment's intrinsic hatred of Donald Trump. It's a hatred that has driven them to sheer insanity, which was nicely stated by the First Lady after seeing Griffin's photo:

When you consider some of the atrocities happening in the world today, a photo opportunity like this is simply wrong and makes you wonder about the mental health of the person who did it.

Mrs. Trump is right. The Establishment has gone mad. It seeks to invalidate a presidential election for the dumbest reason of all—their candidate lost. Since that'll never happen, Establishment knuckleheads have become a mob of nutjobs— the living, breathing embodiment of an old English proverb: "The mob has many heads, but no brains." Somewhere between the election and the inauguration, the Establishment in the United States of America got caught in a time-warping vortex transporting it to a crossroads where medieval days of yore meet the Wild West, a place where lynch mob mentality outweighs the rules of civilized society. Establishment mobs line up with torches ready to exact justice on anyone with whom they disagree, particularly Donald Trump, whom they believe stole the election with the help of the Russians.

The absurdity is truly mind-blowing.

If a mob wants to wield pitchforks, then at least base the decision to do so on reality, not an absurd, unsubstantiated, and, quite frankly, insane conspiracy theory.

There's something unsettling about how the Establishment has devolved into a real-life version of 1931's *Frankenstein* or the old Pace picante sauce commercial where a cowboy, upon hearing his picante sauce came from New York City, calmly, yet firmly, declares, "Get a rope."

The Establishment mob has its noose firmly in hand, and it's headed for the White House. Leading them there? So-called comedians.

Rosie O'Donnell stopped making people laugh a very long time ago. Since then she's waged a vendetta against conservatism and President Trump that borders on pathological obsession.

The two have been feuding since 2006—beginning when, as then-owner of the Miss USA pageant, Trump allowed Miss USA Tara Conner to keep her crown even after reports of her cocaine use and promiscuity. O'Donnell ripped Trump on *The View* and he responded in kind, telling *People* magazine she was "a real loser" and a "woman out of control."

It's been the Hatfields and McCoys ever since.

Two weeks to the day after Trump won the presidential election—two days before Thanksgiving—O'Donnell went after his son, Barron, by suggesting on Twitter the boy suffers from autism:

Barron Trump Autistic? if so—what an amazing opportunity to bring attention to the AUTISM epidemic

She included a YouTube link to a video compilation of Barron Trump clips which implied he displayed "autistic" behavior. Melania Trump threatened the creator of the video with a lawsuit if they didn't remove it—they did.

To use a well-worn cliché, O'Donnell broke the internet. The outrage eruption was swift and sure. Then she backpedaled, claiming a pure motivation; that she just wanted to raise autism awareness.

But when the assailing continued, it raised O'Donnell's ire and she became more aggressive and viler than usual. In fact, when confronted on Twitter by the co-pilot of this book, Dave Erickson, O'Donnell told him, "Go f**k yourself."

This is a comedienne?

There once was a time when children of politicians were off limits. The Establishment made it clear Malia and Sasha Obama, and long before them, Chelsea Clinton, were to be left alone. As is always the case, decorum is tied to political persuasion. If you're the kid of a conservative, duck and cover, you're Establishment prey.

O'Donnell first made a name for herself on the old television talent show *Star Search*. She was genuinely funny.

Her daytime talk show in the late '90s showed a sincere, warm, and engaging person.

What happened?

Over the years, O'Donnell's increasingly erratic diatribes, from The View to Twitter, point to a person lost in the abyss of narcissism and loathing. With the election of Donald Trump as president, any semblance of the talented comedienne was lost to malevolence and an unhealthy fixation.

O'Donnell's Twitter feed is a whirling dervish of negativity. President Trump could find a cure for cancer and she'd complain he was putting oncologists out of work.

If the reason anyone cared about O'Donnell in the first place was because she was a comic, why then, if she no longer tells jokes, is she relevant at all?

O'Donnell should just retire to the alcove under the stairs. Or Rosie, you can always take your own advice and go f**k yourself.

Like O'Donnell, Chelsea Handler is a comedienne who has forgotten that her job, by definition, is to make people laugh. She too swapped real jokes for mean-spirited anti-Trump platitudes, and all but forsaken half of her potential audience. Her eponymous show on Netflix is underperforming—can't imagine why.

Handler is emblematic of the Establishment's whimpering, thin-skinned temperament—seen on full display the day after the election. She struggled not to cry at the start of her show, then gave in as she pontificated on what the Trump victory meant:

I know as a woman, it feels so sexist. I guess the message that I want to spread out to other women is to not give up. Sorry, I hate f**king crying on camera—because this is so important. It's easy to throw in the towel and say that we're gonna leave, or I'm gonna move to Spain. Because I want to move to Spain, I really, really want to move to Spain right now.

We'd like you to move to Spain too.

And everyone in my office is like, "You have a responsibility. You have a voice and you have to use it and you have to be here."

Everyone in her office is right, Handler *does* have a responsibility—it's just not the one they think it is. She has a responsibility to entertain us—not to lecture us about the things she hates about the president half the country voted for.

If you're caught lying on camera three times in a row, if you're referring to a woman's genitalia. Those are non-presidential things . . . un-presidential things.

You know what else is un-presidential? Lying about a private email server in the basement with stored classified correspondence. You know what else is un-presidential? Lying about why four Americans were murdered at the American Embassy in Benghazi, Libya. You know what else is un-presidential? Lying about landing under sniper fire in Bosnia. You know what else is un-presidential? Creating a fake charity for your own enrichment funded by foreign governments and lobbyists buying your influence. You know what else is un-presidential? Laughing at a twelve-year-old rape victim after successfully defending her rapist in court.

There's also a substantial difference between "*referring to a woman's genitalia*" and actually putting a cigar in one. Ask Hillary Clinton whether she considers that act "un-presidential."

Establishment "comedians," and, for that matter, all manner of Establishment "entertainers," seemingly never consider that not everyone agrees with their politics. They abandon jokes for rancor—flagrantly disregarding decorum and respect. Handler posted a photo of herself on Twitter where she's standing topless with her pants pulled down and the words, "Trump is a butt hole" written on her back and—well—butt. She included the caption, "I mean this with the utmost disrespect."

Of course she did. It was the same sort of disrespect Handler showed the First Lady when asked, in a video interview with *Variety*, if she'd ever book Mrs. Trump on her show. Handler answered, "To talk about what? She can barely speak English."

Melania Trump speaks five languages fluently: Slovenian, English, French, German, and Serbian.

Handler is guilty of three primary things with her imbecilic answer: (1) insulting the First Lady, (2) shaming the millions of immigrants in America who have heavy foreign accents, and (3) being stupid enough to assume the First Lady, or the president of the United States, would ever want to appear on a two-bit internet show.

That's Establishment hubris—believing your own hype; believing yourself above others; believing yourself smarter—and that somehow fame is a license to do and say whatever you want without consequence.

Handler doesn't just hold animus for the president and First Lady, she thinks it acceptable to attack his children too.

She has condoned bullying Barron Trump, insulted Eric Trump after he announced he and his wife were expecting their first child, made fun of Tiffany Trump for not seeing her dad that much when she was growing up, and ripped into Ivanka Trump because Handler thinks she should do more to influence her father on women's issues: "I'm like, 'You need to tell that f**king *sshole this is an unacceptable way to treat women; we're moving backwards!'"

Chelsea Handler isn't a comedienne; she's a bully.

It's fitting she and Sarah Silverman are friends—they share the same Establishment self-righteousness and arrogance, blinding them to their own cluelessness and fostering obnoxious behavior. Silverman thinks it's smart comedy to dress as Adolf Hitler, which she did on *Conan*, and compare our president with the soulless Nazi monster who killed six million Jews. As a Jewish person herself, you'd think Silverman would know better than to reduce an atrocity like the Holocaust to a prop for a two-bit comedy bit mocking the president.

This "comedienne" has mocked Jesus, Christians, and the children of Britney Spears when they were barely toddlers, insulted the transgendered, appeared in blackface, made racist jokes, called for a military coup to overthrow the Trump White House, referred to anyone that questioned the health of Hillary Clinton as "f**king *ssholes," and at an anti-Trump "Tax March" in New York City screamed, "Show us your f**king taxes, you emotional child!"

He's the emotional child?

Nastiness like that is to be expected from an Establishment whiner like Silverman who, before she supported Hillary Clinton, went all in for Bernie Sanders—the socialist who didn't earn a full-time paycheck until he was forty, has never had a full-time private sector job, yet somehow owns three homes. How supportive of socialism would Silverman be if someone started dipping into her reported $12-million net worth to give ne'er-do-wells a bunch of free stuff?

A week or so after Donald Trump won the presidential election, Silverman reacted in the sort of over-the-top, dramatic, fear-stoking way we've come to expect from Establishment sore losers. She lamented on Twitter, "For a lot of people, this is the Great Depression, but this time it's emotional & physical. Our bodies r breaking down w fear & rage . . ."

Bodies are breaking down? (insert eye roll here) Perhaps Silverman's body, and those of her Establishment cronies, were breaking down with fear and rage—they're spineless lemmings—but the rest of us feel stronger than ever. Those who truly love America don't cower when a politician with whom they disagree is elected. Their bodies don't break down. People who truly love America now wake up feeling hopeful, for after eight years of division stoked by a Marxist administration, there's the promise of limitless possibility provided by a new president.

CHAPTER 16

ISN'T LATE-NIGHT COMEDY SUPPOSED TO BE FUNNY?

Johnny Carson will always be the undisputed king of late-night television. For thirty years, he held court over the crown jewel of NBC: *The Tonight Show*. Though extraordinarily well read, intelligent, and well aware of the issues of the day, Carson never went on-air and tried to be anything other than what he was—a late-night talk show host and comedian. He wasn't a pundit. Carson told jokes. He didn't opine, for good reason, explaining to the *New Yorker* in 1978, "That would hurt me as an entertainer, which is what I am."

Carson knew his role.

Contrast that with the late-night landscape of today.

Lighthearted entertainment isn't the goal: eviscerating President Trump is. Late-night television is an aural onslaught of Establishment hosts pushing *their* political views onto America. But shouting into an echo chamber serves to do nothing more than feed the already oversized egos of hosts who believe themselves intellectual elites. To the Trump haters who watch these buffoons, they're hilarious. To the rest of us, they're unwatchable.

When Carson ruled the late-night airwaves, there was a smorgasbord of low-hanging comic fruit coming from Pennsylvania Avenue. During those thirty years, the occupants of the Oval Office included LBJ, Nixon, Ford, Carter, Reagan, and the first George Bush. Talk about meaty lambs ready for slaughter. But Carson never went low. He joked but wasn't mean-spirited. As Carson once told *Life* magazine, "There are times when I would like to express a view on the air . . . But I'm on TV five nights a week; I have nothing to gain by it and everything to lose." And, that is why Carson was the king of late night for three decades. He understood what today's hosts don't: people watch late-night comedy shows to be entertained, not lectured. Carson wasn't so shortsighted as to alienate half the country by beating viewers over the head with his political views—or verbally ravaging a president for whom those viewers may have voted.

Late night now is a cacophony of bombast. *The Late Show with Stephen Colbert* is no more than a nightly skewering of President Trump by a smug host. Colbert has sixty minutes of valuable airtime and all he and his high-priced writers can come up with are demeaning jokes about the president. It's not clever. It's lazy. Maureen Callahan at the *New York Post* put it best: "Stephen Colbert used to parody a blowhard—now he is one."

To be fair, Colbert isn't just a blowhard, he's a very talented man wasting his talent dishing filthy hyperbole grounded in an unhealthy obsession with destroying the president. Why else would he walk out onto his stage at the Ed Sullivan Theater on May 2, 2017, and deliver the most repulsive, disrespectful monologue directed at a sitting president in the history of television?

Colbert launched his verbal offensive—or better yet, his offensive verbal—after President Trump dismissed the host of CBS' *Face the Nation*, John Dickerson, from the Oval Office when Dickerson questioned him about the claims he'd made about being wiretapped by Barack Obama. Colbert looked at the camera and spoke directly to President Trump:

John Dickerson has way too much dignity to trade insults with the president of the United States to his face. But I, sir, am no John Dickerson. Let me introduce you to something we call "the Tiffany Way." When you insult one member of the CBS family, you insult us all. Bazinga!

Then Colbert's crude, albeit searing, personal attack of the president really began:

Mr. Trump, your presidency—I love your presidency. I call it "Disgrace the Nation." You're not the POTUS, you're the BLOTUS. You're the glutton with the button. You're a regular "Gorge" Washington. You're the presi-dunce, but you're turning into a real prick-tator. Sir, you attract more skinheads than free Rogaine.

You have more people marching against you than cancer. You talk like a sign language gorilla who got hit in the head.

In fact, the only thing your mouth is good for is being Vladimir Putin's c**k holster.

Your presidential library is gonna be a kids' menu and a couple of Jugs magazines. The only thing smaller than your hands is your tax returns. And you can take that any way you want.

This is how a comic satirist on a major television network speaks to the president of the United States? In front of three million viewers? On the "Tiffany" network?

Where's the outrage? Where's the consequence? Had a late-night host said the same of Barack Obama, a mob armed with torches and pitchforks would be gathered in front of the network's headquarters, and they wouldn't stop until the host was either fired or lynched.

Not with Colbert though. Disgustingly homophobic inferences directed at the president are acceptable when you're an Establishment mouthpiece—especially when you have the support of equally tone-deaf sycophants.

Stephen Colbert—you, sir, are no Johnny Carson.

In the entertainment bastions of East and West Coast Establishment thinking, it's considered sport to bad-mouth our president in boorish fashion. The mindset of these shows is, to paraphrase the late Rowdy Roddy Piper, "We came to demean the president and chew gum, and we're all out of gum."

HBO's *Last Week Tonight with John Oliver* is, for all intents and purposes, host John Oliver screaming for half an hour about how bad he thinks our president is. Dude, no one is making you stay here. Feel free to jump on the red-eye back to your native England. Certainly, Prime Minister May generates an ample supply of fodder for your unhinged ruminations.

Comedy Central's Trevor Noah is no better. The host of *The Daily Show* routinely mocks conservatives, their policies, and of course, President Trump. What's particularly charming about Noah's incessant whining is he's from South Africa, a country where the economy is falling apart thanks to years of socialist policy. Trevor, you can complain all you want about this capitalist country in which you earn millions of dollars, but we'd prefer if you just said, "Thanks."

Viewers of *Late Night with Seth Meyers* and *Jimmy Kimmel Live!* don't need to think very hard about which side of the political fence their hosts stand. Although Kimmel did share a hearty laugh with guest Tim Allen when the sitcom star and comedian likened Hollywood's prevailing intolerance with Nazi fascism: "You've got to be real careful around here, you'll get beat up if you don't believe what everybody believes. It's like '30s Germany."

But poor Jimmy Fallon at *The Tonight Show*. Like Johnny Carson before him—who set the benchmark for how a host is to conduct their show—Fallon is deliberately apolitical and he's been relentless criticized as a result.

The zenith of the criticism was also its genesis: when Donald Trump was a guest on *The Tonight Show* a couple of months before the election. Fallon's interview was void of heavy-handed questioning or "gotcha" moments. It also included Fallon doing what everyone in America has wanted to do since the '80s—he playfully tousled Trump's hair.

The segment was lighthearted, good fun, and entertaining—everything a late-night comedy show is supposed to be. But a vicious Establishment, hell-bent on the destruction of Donald Trump, wouldn't have it. They rebuked Fallon for weeks.

But of all today's late-night hosts, Fallon is the only one who gets it—the one who understands it isn't smart to alienate half your audience by pushing partisan politics (or alliteration). As he told *The New York Times*, "I tossed and turned for a couple of weeks, but I have to make people laugh. People that voted for Trump watch my show as well."

Amen.

Johnny Carson set a standard for late-night hosts, and thankfully, today, one measures up. There might just be hope for late night after all.

SECTION 5

MEDIA SHMEDIA

CHAPTER 17

WHAT'S WITH THE POLITICS? I JUST WANT TO WATCH A GAME.

Like late-night television, sports broadcasts are supposed to be an area of escape—where we pop suds and bask in "the constant variety of sport; the thrill of victory and the agony of defeat; the human drama of athletic competition." At least that's how it used to be when we had ABC's *Wide World of Sports* on Saturday afternoons.

Sports give a needed breather from the punditry and anti-Americanism coursing through the veins of most twenty-four-hour cable news.

Well, it *used* to.

In the twenty-first century, the Establishment pushes its ideology everywhere. Like an Orwellian tapeworm, it seeps its way into every nook, cranny, and crevice of society—including sports.

Who wants to hear a spiel on gun control during halftime of an NFL game? Nobody. But in 2012 we got one anyway.

On NBC's *Sunday Night Football*, Bob Costas lectured us about gun control—during a *sports* broadcast—because that week Kansas City Chiefs linebacker Jovan Belcher got drunk and murdered his girlfriend with a .40-caliber handgun. Belcher then drove to the Chiefs' practice complex and killed himself in the parking lot while the team's general manager watched in horror. According to Costas—the Establishment sage, "If Jovan Belcher didn't possess a gun, he and Kasandra Perkins would both be alive today."

How could Costas even know that? Is he clairvoyant?

In addition to a self-righteous sports announcer preaching the dangers of guns, do I need a sports network to tell me it takes the same courage to come out as "transgendered" as it does to fight through brain cancer?

Is this what we want from the sports desk? Establishment politics?

I just want to eat hot wings and watch a game.

But there is one network that transcends all the rest in its unadulterated politicization of sports: ESPN. The self-proclaimed "Worldwide Leader in Sports" is slowly killing itself with Establishment politics. The network has weaved political discourse so thoroughly into its culture, viewers have checked out bigly, and combined with their ridiculous overspending for broadcast rights and a shrinking subscriber base, ESPN has real problems.

It might be an overstatement to put the lion's share of blame on politics, although the Establishment positions ESPN holds as a network, and those of some of their on-air talent, have turned off viewers who want the simple joy of sports sans politics. ESPN's ratings were down by double digits from 2016–2017, the network has laid off hundreds of employees, including several high-profile on-air personalities, and in a survey by Barrett Sports Media, a whopping 61 percent of the participants said ESPN has a left-leaning agenda. To make matters worse, the survey also found a combined 91 percent of the participants say they consume ESPN's content less or no longer enjoy it.

Nine out of every ten people no longer enjoy ESPN content or enjoy it less. Among the reasons cited by the survey participants was, "Too much focus on hot take shows with a left-leaning agenda and less on making sports fun and neutral."

Wow! If anything should have triggered the ESPN NORAD command center to go to DEFCON 1, this was it. Incredibly, the network disregarded this *extremely loud* distress signal from its viewers. Establishment media prefers to live in denial than to accept they're not as "down the middle" as they claim to be.

At a shareholder meeting in March of 2017, the CEO of the Walt Disney Company (which owns ESPN), Bob Iger, addressed an accusation the network showed left-leaning bias in its on-air coverage of Donald Trump. His response? "The charge that ESPN is exhibiting significant political bias is just a complete exaggeration."

When you've got 61 percent of your audience saying the network leans left, you really need to pay attention. But it's just like the Establishment to embrace a total lack of self-awareness and to ignore contrary data so it can continue to push its agenda.

And these people can't figure out why Hillary Clinton lost the election.

Also, why is a *sports* network talking about Donald Trump at all?

ESPN gives a platform to NFL players who espouse Establishment views—players who think quarterback Colin Kaepernick is some sort of civil rights martyr and hero. He's a guy who famously refused to stand for the national anthem before games because, "I am not going to stand up to show pride in a flag for a country that oppresses black people and people of color." A country that "oppresses black people"? Perhaps Kaepernick didn't hear, a black man was elected president of the United States—twice.

Kaepernick signed a contract with the 49ers for $126 million. The average hardworking American will never, ever, ever, ever earn that kind of money in the entirety of their lifetime. But Kaepernick is an oppressed black man. Oh, wait a second, that's not accurate either. Kaepernick is half *white*. His biological father was black, his biological mother, white. He was raised by a well-to-do white couple that adopted him. So, the whole oppressed black man thing—yeah, not a lot of that happening right there.

In a country that's given him so much, Kaepernick thumbed his nose at "the Star-Spangled Banner"—basically flipping the bird to every man and woman who fought and died for our flag. Would we expect anything less from a guy who showed up to a news conference wearing a T-shirt emblazoned with a picture of Fidel Castro?

None of this stopped an ESPN personality from vehemently defending Kaepernick. When the QB remained unemployed throughout the whole of the 2017 free agent season, Bomani Jones, a co-host of one of the network's afternoon shows, *Highly Questionable*, wrote a piece for the ESPN-owned website The Undefeated. He stridently suggested that anyone who cited "distraction" as the reason for teams not signing Kaepernick were disingenuous—because Kaepernick said he'd resume standing for the national anthem. Instead, Jones claimed, the real reason Kaepernick went unsigned was—wait for it, wait for it—racism!

> *We could address what makes it so difficult to tease out exactly why Kaepernick remains jobless—it's hard to tell if he's being treated as an unruly black man, or just as a black quarterback.*

So, all thirty-two NFL teams colluded to keep Kaepernick from playing because every NFL team executive is racist? Sure, and Russia swayed the election for Donald Trump. It's just like the Establishment to pull out the race card when there's no good hand to play.

The host of ESPN's *First Take*, Stephen A. Smith, likes to play the race card too. When quarterback Robert Griffin III—at the time playing for the Washington Redskins—was benched in favor of his backup, the white Kirk Cousins, according to Smith, it wasn't because Griffin's play stunk like three-day-old raw chicken, it was because he's black.

Ironically, on *First Take* a few years earlier, Smith's co-host at the time, Rob Parker, idiotically asked whether Griffin was even black at all:

> My question is, and it's just a straight, honest question: Is he a brother, or is he a cornball brother? He's not really. He's black, he does his thing, but he's not really down with the cause. He's not one of us. He's kind of black, but he's not really like the kind of guy you really want to hang out with.

Parker expressed that Griffin needed to meet black stereotypes before he could accept him.

> We all know he has a white fiancée. Then there was all this talk about he's a Republican, which there's no information at all.

Does Parker need a black man to say "Yass, Massuh" every time he's told to do something to prove he's black? How disgustingly archaic is he? Parker also had the sheer gall—or ignorance—to suggest you can't be black and be a Republican.

ESPN fired this Neanderthal about a month later.

How about when Tony Kornheiser, on ESPN 980 radio in Washington, DC, likened the Tea Party to ISIS and asked,

"Are they starting a caliphate?" He's still employed by ESPN. Any question there's an anti-conservative bias over there?

Kornheiser suffered no repercussions, yet Sage Steele did. Shortly after ESPN issued a new policy limiting the on-air commentary of its talent, they pulled the conservative Christian reporter and host from her plum assignment on *NBA Countdown* and replaced her with the unabashedly liberal Michelle Beadle. Steele was reassigned to another show, but ESPN could not have been happy with the conservative views she's expressed on the air over the years. Steele had:

- complained about airport protestors of President Trump's travel ban.

- criticized Colin Kaepernick and other NFL players who wouldn't stand for the national anthem.

- cut off an interview at the NBA All-Star Celebrity Game with a singer who started spouting leftist political opinions.

- claimed the worst racism she ever encountered came from other black people.

That Steele is still employed by ESPN is a minor miracle given how they've treated conservative on-air talent in the past. Consider Curt Schilling. The former Major League pitching great is a six-time MLB All Star, three-time World

Series champion, a World Series MVP, and to ESPN's chagrin, a conservative.

Schilling used to be one of ESPN's highest-paid analysts. But once he posted a meme on Facebook responding to the North Carolina bathroom bill, ESPN pulled him from the mound and sent him to the showers.

The sad thing is, what Schilling wrote is true:

> A man is a man no matter what they call themselves. I don't care what they are, who they sleep with, men's room was designed for the penis, women's not so much. Now you need laws telling us differently? Pathetic.

The corresponding photo was of a large, unattractive man dressed in women's clothes with the caption, "Let him into the restroom with your daughter or else you're a narrow-minded, judgmental, unloving racist bigot who needs to die!!!" To the Establishment, that's horrifying. To the rest of us, that's hilarious! And to ESPN, it's non-inclusive.

In the wake of his firing, Schilling went on *The Dan Patrick Show*, on NBC then, and peeled back the veil revealing the true motive of ESPN's new commentary policy and the anti-conservative culture of ESPN as a network:

> I think what the memo meant to say was, "If you're not liberal and you're not a Democrat, do not stray from sports." . . . The other thing that really jumped out at me was people would talk,

you know, the green room where everybody
hangs out, it's the ESPN version of the locker
room. A lot of times people would be like, they
would come up to me and whisper, "Hey man,
I'm with ya, I'm a Republican," as if we were
the secret card-carrying members of some group
that couldn't be, the "those who shall not be
named." The inclusiveness is inclusive as long
as you are pointing in the same direction.

It's clear, ESPN supports the Establishment agenda. At its annual awards show, *The ESPYS*, the network gave its highest honor, the Arthur Ashe Courage Award, to a man who had the courage to have his penis removed—Caitlyn née Bruce Jenner.

Sure, we get it. It takes guts to be an American icon, an Olympic hero, the archetypical man and to stand in front of the world and confess how you've been struggling with sexual identity and want to be a woman. My god, that must have been tough. Sincerely. But for ESPN to put cause célèbre over real courage is so appallingly distasteful.

Lauren Hill was but a teenager when she was told she had just a few months to live—she'd been diagnosed with a rare form of pediatric brain cancer, and it was inoperable. But the nineteen-year-old college freshman had a dream—a dream of playing basketball for Mount Joseph University in Cincinnati. With help from the NCAA, which moved a previously scheduled game up on the schedule to accommodate her failing health, Hill fulfilled her dream. It couldn't have been easy. The tumor in her brain caused excruciating headaches, and the medicinal treatment—extreme nausea. Yet, there was Lauren Hill, on a basketball court courageously inspiring others to never quit.

It was a cold November night in Ohio. But when word spread statewide about this brave young lady, so many people wanted to see the game with Hiram College, it was moved to a bigger venue at Xavier University to accommodate the ten thousand who showed up. And what they saw was one of the bravest, most inspirational feats of that season or any other.

Lauren Hill played four games during the 2014 season, before the cancer finally took its toll. She passed away five months after that first game, but not before fulfilling her other dream: raising awareness of diffuse intrinsic pontine glioma, or DIPG. In her final months on Earth, fighting through a pain we can't imagine, Hill helped to raise more than $1 million for DIPG cancer research.

That's pretty award-worthy, don't ya think?

In 2001, after the planes hit the Twin Towers, a patriotic twenty-year-old man named Noah Galloway committed to serve his country and he enlisted in the United States Army. It wasn't long before the good-looking young man from Alabama was in Iraq with the 101st Airborne Division. One night, during his second tour of duty, Galloway was driving a Humvee when it ran over a roadside bomb. The explosion blew off one of Galloway's arms and a leg.

After understandably sinking into the depths of depression afterward, and getting wildly out of shape, Galloway joined a gym and pushed himself to conquer his handicap—even with prosthetics. The man is ripped, more than most people who have all their extremities. Galloway is now an extreme athlete who competes in grueling endurance competitions, CrossFit events, long-distance running races, and, as you may have seen, season 20 of *Dancing with the Stars*.

Galloway established the "No Excuses Charitable Fund" which raises money and awareness for organizations that inspire people to achieve better health and supports wounded veterans.

From fighting evil in Iraq to fighting unimaginable pain, Galloway is courage personified. The man has a Purple Heart, but isn't good enough for an ESPY?

As far as ESPN is concerned, neither a war hero who overcame severe injuries to become a world-class athlete, nor a teenage basketball player who battled brain cancer with dignity and grace, is as brave as a cross-dressing gold medalist.

ESPN, at this point, who are you kidding? Change your name to MSESPN, push your Establishment views, and let someone else do the sports.

I just want to eat hot wings and watch a game.

CHAPTER 18

#FAKENEWS

Sorry folks, but if I would have relied on the Fake News of CNN, NBC, ABC, CBS, washpost or nytimes, I would have had ZERO chance winning WH.

–President Donald J. Trump
Twitter post, June 6, 2017

There is literally no story you can believe if it comes from the Establishment news media.

Period.

Today's national media aren't arbiters of truth—they're the propaganda arm of the Democratic National Committee, single-minded of purpose: to use disinformation disguised as "journalism" to destroy the presidency of Donald Trump.

Few of the line-towing minions working in national news consider flyover America much. From the comfort of the ivory towers overlooking New York, Washington, DC, Los Angeles, and Atlanta, they gaze contemptuously at people they perceive to be "uneducated, racist rednecks" too stupid to see through the ruse of bogus "journalism." What these Establishment bootlickers fail to consider is (1) Middle America isn't comprised of uneducated, racist rednecks, and (2) the media moxie of Trump's America.

In 2004, after Dan Rather went on CBS's *60 Minutes* and reported a bogus story about President George W. Bush's service in the Texas National Guard—which relied on fabricated documents—Rather, and his producer, Mary Mapes, were vilified once the story unceremoniously fell apart. Sure, conservative America knew it was journalistic malfeasance, but there wasn't yet a coined universal term that accurately described the subversive fraud committed by so-called journalists—that all changed with Donald Trump.

"Fake news."

President Trump may not have coined the term, but he certainly made it ubiquitous.

CNN, NBC, ABC, CBS, MSNBC, the *New York Times*, the *Washington Post, The Hill, POLITCO,* Reuters, Associated Press, *Los Angeles Times, Huffington Post, BuzzFeed, Slate, VICE News*—these are just some of the outlets pushing false and (or) misleading news stories about the Trump administration. The list of fake news propagandists is almost as long as Hillary Clinton's list of excuses for why she lost the election.

The Establishment media landscape nowadays is largely occupied by irresponsible reporters peddling a predetermined narrative with a ratings-obsessed, reality-TV mindset in which the search for truth isn't paramount.

For the eight years of the Obama administration, the Establishment abandoned all journalistic enterprise. The arming of Mexican drug lords through Operation Fast and Furious; conservative groups targeted by the IRS; backroom dealings leading to energy loan guarantees that screwed taxpayers when "green energy" companies went belly-up; spying on journalists, like James Rosen of Fox News—the Establishment media's take on these and other Obama misdeeds? Move along! Nothing to see here!

For Obama? Turn a blind eye

For Trump? Go for the kill.

But these aren't the conspiratorial musings of a conservative mind. In fact, they were proven true by one of the very foundations of the Establishment itself: Harvard University.

The Harvard Kennedy School's Shorenstein Center on Media, Politics and Public Policy analyzed the news coverage of President Trump's first one hundred days in office—it found bias against the administration so vast and negative coverage so profound, it is unrivaled by coverage of any other president in American history.

The study was based on analysis of television and print news coverage, both in America and abroad. Domestically, they analyzed the main newscasts of CBS, NBC, CNN, Fox News, and NBC, and the print editions of *The New York Times*, the *Wall Street Journal*, and the *Washington Post*. The overseas outlets were Germany's ARD and the UK's BBC and *Financial Times*.

Not one of them had coverage found to be more positive than negative—no, not even Fox.

In looking at the "tone" of the news coverage during Trump's first hundred days, the study concluded:

CNN: 93 percent negative
NBC: 93 percent negative
CBS: 91 percent negative
NYT: 87 percent negative
TWP: 83 percent negative
WSJ: 70 percent negative
Fox: 52 percent negative

The overseas outlets were overwhelmingly negative as well. In Germany, the coverage was nearly 100 percent negative.

When President Trump claims the media is hostile, he's not being petulant. It is!

One collateral result of the study is it proves Fox News to be the fair and balanced outlet it promotes itself as, and not the Trump cheerleader the Establishment claims. The tone of Fox's Trump coverage at 52/48 (negative/positive) is a near even split. So, the next time some snowflake blathers on about how Fox is biased for Trump, you tell 'em, "Take your fake news back over to CNN."

CNN, of course, would have you believe it's a model of objectivity, but another study, this one by the Media Research Center (MRC), found that on a given day, CNN is unflinchingly committed to anti-Trump coverage.

For the study, MRC reviewed one day of CNN's programming—May 12, 2017—beginning at 4:00 a.m. ET and ending at 11:00 p.m. ET. It found that CNN dedicated 92 percent of its coverage for the day to Donald Trump. The rest of the day's news got a total of 68 minutes' coverage. In twenty hours of programming, the self-proclaimed "most trusted name in news" found just barely more than an hour for actual news not involving Donald Trump.

CNN's guests that day? MRC counted a staggering ninety-six Trump critics to just seven pro-Trump guests.

Yo, CNN. Obsessed much?

To turn a phrase, the proof is in the pudding—the "objective" news network has a top to bottom commitment to undermining Donald Trump.

CNN's contempt for the president couldn't be more boldfaced than a tweet by one of its former show hosts, Reza Aslan.

In the aftermath of a terror attack in London, where radical Islamic militants killed seven people and injured several dozen more, President Trump, on Twitter (of course), reiterated the importance of a temporary travel ban from certain countries in maintaining the safety of the country:

> We need to be smart, vigilant and tough. We need the courts to give us back our rights. We need the Travel Ban as an extra level of safety!

> We must stop being politically correct and get down to the business of security for our people. If we don't get smart it will only get worse.

Aslan's tweeted response?

This piece of sh*t is not just an embarrassment to America and a stain on the presidency. He's an embarrassment on humankind.

Donald Trump wants to keep Americans safe, and CNN's self-proclaimed "scholar of religion" calls him an expletive and a "stain on the presidency"? What does that make Aslan? We already know he's a left-wing Muslim activist. We already know his Twitter timeline is a string of profanity-laced insults aimed at conservatives—although he falsely claimed in an "apology" it was out of character for him to respond in a derogatory fashion.

CNN's response at first was to say Aslan wasn't a CNN employee, only that he hosted a show that aired on the network. However, a week or so later, CNN booted him and cancelled production on Aslan's documentary series, *Believer.*

Hostility is what happens when Establishment media is unconditionally terrified of an administration it cannot control—and hostility manifests as fake news. Aslan might be an *sshole but at least he wasn't staging a story—like his colleagues did in London the day after the London terror attack.

Behind-the-scenes footage posted on Twitter showed CNN correspondent Becky Anderson and someone else directing pro-Muslim demonstrators where to stand as she prepared for a live shot. The narrative CNN was apparently attempting to craft was that Muslims in London are anti-extremist.

About a dozen or so people, mostly women in hijabs, stood in CNN's shot holding signs that said, "#TurnToLove," "#LoveWillWin," and "#ISISEqualsEnemiesOfIslam"— because as we've already noted, few things are as potent in fighting evil than a hashtag.

When Sean Hannity of Fox News saw the video, he decimated CNN that night on *Hannity*:

> *It's two and a half minutes. You literally see the guy in the white shirt over there. He says, "Oh, this is where the mark is. This is where you stand. This is where we want you to stand" . . . Then they get the shot in, telling them where to go. "All right, time to put up your signs." It's almost like, "'All right, quiet on the set! Quiet on the set! Alright? Ready? Fake news in 3, 2, 1. Action! Go!"*

CNN denied the crew staged anything, calling the implication "nonsense." You know what else is nonsense? That denial. CNN knows as well as anyone in the news business, if you tell people in a protest where to stand, that's staging.

Fake news arrives in all manner of ways. A producer or reporter shapes a narrative by bending a fact, ignoring a fact, or removing the context, or they might do what NBC did and pull the old Steve Urkel "Did I do that?" trick.

In the days leading up to the premiere of Megyn Kelly's new show, *Sunday Night with Megyn Kelly*, which featured a sit-down interview with Russian president Vladimir Putin, NBC falsely promoted a Kelly "exclusive" that all but confirmed President Trump had been in cahoots with the Russians! The NBC tweet read:

> *EXCLUSIVE: Putin does not deny having compromising information on President Trump in an interview with @MegynKelly.*

The one problem with this? Putin *did* deny having compromising information. NBC lied. In the interview itself, there's Putin calling the allegation "another load of nonsense" and asking the same question of Kelly that conservatives ask the Establishment media every day: "Have you all lost your minds over there?" NBC was forced to retract the lie a short time after it posted the first tweet:

> *CORRECTION: Putin denies having compromising information about President Trump, calls it nonsense.*

Oops.

But that bit of fake news to pimp Kelly's new show wasn't sufficient for NBC, so there's Kelly tossing another falsehood like a grenade, only this one exploded in her hand. Sitting across from Putin, Kelly claimed that "all seventeen of the

United States' intelligence agencies have concluded that the Russians did interfere with our election."

The problem with that statement—it's not true.

NBC knew it wasn't true. Just a few weeks earlier at a Senate hearing, the former director of national intelligence, James Clapper, deliberately corrected the erroneous number, that it was *three* agencies, not seventeen.

But in the world of the Establishment, it didn't matter. By then, the rest of the Establishment media had already spread the fake news story like a virus. For them, successfully concocting the mere *appearance* of impropriety is a win.

NBC's ugly sister, MSNBC, did the same thing just before Christmas in 2016 when host Stephanie Ruhle falsely claimed Fox News held its annual holiday party at the recently opened Trump International Hotel in Washington. Not only did the president's hotel *not* host the Fox party—Fox hadn't even had its party yet.

Ruhle had to apologize on-air for the false accusation.

But if there's a gilded lining to fake news, it's that it turns the Establishment into Wile E. Coyote on the endless quest to destroy the Roadrunner. Acme delivers woefully malfunctioning instruments of torture, and the diabolical plan ends with either a 4,000-foot plunge off a canyon ledge or an anvil to the face.

It happened throughout the 2016 election season. One skewed poll result after another, all aimed at misleading voters that Donald Trump had no chance of winning the presidency. The Acme bomb blew up mightily in the Establishment's face on November 8, 2016.

But their failed efforts only enraged and emboldened them.

No story is too big nor too small to fabricate.

The New England Patriots, as is tradition for Super Bowl–winning teams, paid a visit to the White House, where the team met President Trump and they all posed for a group photo on the South Portico. The *New York Times* soon tweeted a pair of photos comparing this Patriots visit with their 2015 visit with then-President Obama. The photos were clear: the group of attendees was substantially larger for the visit with Obama. But as Keith Morrison on *Dateline NBC* might ask, "Or was it?"

Upon seeing the photos online, the New England Patriots organization itself called out the *Times* on Twitter:

> *These photos lack context. Facts: In 2015, over*
> *40 football staff were on the stairs. In 2017,*
> *they were seated on the South Lawn.*

The *Times* deliberately didn't show the complete 2017 photo with the Patriots staff on the lawn. Fact is, the size of the delegation was about the same for both visits. As is the Establishment modus operandi once it gets caught, a mea culpa by the *Times* sports editor followed:

> *Bad tweet by me. Terrible tweet. I wish I could*
> *say it's complicated, but no, this one is pretty*
> *straightforward: I'm an idiot. It was my idea, it*
> *was my execution, it was my blunder. I made*

a decision in about four minutes that clearly
warranted much more time.

Boom goes the dynamite! (Supplied by Acme, of course.)
The Establishment media can't be trusted. It's easy to see why President Trump tweets as often as he does—he's forced to bypass a dishonest media to ensure his message is delivered to the American public unfiltered.

Most Americans know the Establishment media feeds them fake news—almost two-thirds of the country, according to a Harvard-Harris poll, believe fake news is prevalent in mainstream media. As far as news on social media is concerned, forget about it—90 percent of us believe it's mostly fake.

The Establishment can't help itself. It's on a mission. Regardless of importance they'll fake any story. Whether it's as seemingly insignificant as a team picture at the White House, a Fox holiday party, falsely claiming a temporary vetting is a "Muslim ban"—or truly substantive issues like alleged Russian interference in a US election, the dismissal of FBI chief James Comey, or reporting things like the *Wall Street Journal* did—"Saudi Arabia and UAE Pledge $100 Million to Ivanka's Women Entrepreneurs Fund," when Ivanka doesn't even have such a thing—you simply cannot trust that the news being presented by the Establishment media isn't fake.

If they had any integrity, a news network would hire Norm Macdonald as their anchor and have him open the newscast the way he did in the '90s on *Saturday Night Live*'s "Weekend Update"—"Good evening, I'm Norm Macdonald and now the fake news."

CHAPTER 19

THE RUSSIANS ARE COMING! THE RUSSIANS ARE COMING!

Well, he [Vladimir Putin] certainly interfered in our election and it was clear he interfered to hurt me and helped my opponent.

–Hillary Clinton to CNN's Christiane Amanpour

If you gave any credence to Establishment propaganda for the better part of the year following Donald Trump's victory, you'd have believed Vladimir Putin was running a fiendishly diabolical plan of election sabotage from an underground super-lair using the pseudonym Ernst Stavro Blofeld while spearheading SPECTRE's march toward world domination.

The Establishment asserted Russian interference stole the election from Hillary Clinton—a claim so patently absurd it's cartoonish. Putin went from world leader to Bond villain.

Clinton and the Establishment apologists grasp at anything on which to put blame for her election loss: uneducated voters, fake news, WikiLeaks, the DNC, the RNC, incorrect polling data, sexism, social media, cable news, Tom and Jerry, ill-fitting pantsuits, former FBI director James Comey, and, of course, the Russians, led by Putin.

The Establishment media spent so much time pushing Russian interference it spent weekends eating borscht and bathing in vats of Stolichnaya. But here's the thing: Russia didn't interfere in the American presidential election. Clinton lost it all by herself.

The Establishment needed a scapegoat. How else to pacify the humiliation of knowing you lost an "un-losable" election to a businessman/reality television star with zero political experience? That's when fake news launched into hyperdrive and ended up in what *Vox* dubbed the "Russiasphere."

Establishment media pushed scores of stories from all corners—each increasingly nonsensical—which ultimately pointed to the same basic allegation: the Kremlin wanted Donald Trump to be the president of the United States, so it worked *with* him in a nefarious scheme to discredit Hillary Clinton with voters, thus sending her voters over to Trump.

This would be laughable it if wasn't so sad, and frankly, downright irresponsible.

Besides, as secretary of state, didn't Clinton sell one-fifth of America's uranium rights to Russia? In return, didn't Russia give her slush-fund foundation enough money to fill up a stadium-sized parking lot with cash-laden armored trucks? It seems Crooked Hillary and Russia were very good to each other. Why would it sabotage her?

It makes no sense. Establishment thought rarely does.

The purveyors of fake news, buoyed by unnamed "anonymous" sources, attempted to delegitimize the Trump presidency by spreading "collusion" stories that were tenuous at best.

Leading the charge of the tinfoil hat-wearing Establishment disinformation posse was a British blogger named Louise Mensch. Her site, *Patribotics*—with its tagline: "Exposing Vladimir Putin's War in America"—is a collection of entries too farcical to be taken seriously. In one, she asserts that Carter Page, one of President Trump's foreign policy advisors, flew to Moscow, under Trump's authorization, and asked the Russian government to hack the US election, and in exchange, Trump would change American policy to be more favorable to Putin. The fun part of this tale? Mensch claims Trump pre-recorded the request and Page played the tape for the Russians.

Patribotics is a plethora of half-baked conjecture—including a series of events that has Anthony Wiener and the former head of the FBI, James Comey, in the role of marionettes manipulated by dastardly Russians out to destroy Clinton's chances come Election Day. It goes something like this:

- Attorney General Jeff Sessions is a "Russian partisan."

- Carter Page is a "spy."

- There are Russian "moles" working inside the FBI.

- These moles either "found or planted" emails related to the FBI investigation into Clinton's private email server onto Anthony Weiner's laptop—emails sent by his wife Huma Abedin, the vice chair of the Clinton campaign.

- When Weiner exchanged text messages with what he thought was a fifteen-year-old girl, the girl was really a Russian hacker—and the entire incident was part of a Russian plot to get the Clinton emails back into the news.

- Russian moles had the FBI field office "suddenly find" the Clinton emails on Weiner's computer.

- Upon the revelation of the email discovery, the Russian moles pressured Comey to write a letter informing Congress of the FBI investigation into whether the emails contained classified information—and, once the public got wind of it, this would "thereby spin the election to Trump."

There you have it—Donald Trump is president because James Comey caved to Russian moles.

Ask Clinton herself. In an interview, she spoke her belief that she'd be president had Comey not written that letter to Congress and reopened the investigation into her private server. Clinton and the Establishment media needed a patsy to blame. They chose two: Comey and Russia. It's like the president tweeted, "The Democrats made up and pushed the Russian story as an excuse for running a terrible campaign. Big advantage in Electoral College and lost!"

Nailed it.

Twenty-five days after the president's inauguration, the *New York Times* published an article with this headline: "Trump Campaign Aides Had Repeated Contacts with Russian Intelligence." It was a bold proclamation to be sure. The problem? It wasn't true.

Three and a half months later, when Comey appeared before the Senate Intelligence Committee, Arkansas senator Tom Cotton asked specifically about the *Times* article, "Would it be fair to characterize that story as almost entirely wrong?" Comey's answer? "Yes."

The Establishment media breathlessly weaves tales of Russian collusion through television news, online sites, newspapers, magazines, blogs, radio, and podcasts, though there never has been even a scintilla of evidence linking Donald Trump to the Russians. They shout it from the rooftops with bold proclamations that are nothing more than fables concocted by a dishonest media. More examples:

- *The Guardian*: "Donald Trump Is Under Investigation for Ties to Russia. What Happens Now?"

- *Huffington Post*: "Schumer: Delay Gorsuch while Trump Is Under FBI Investigation"

- *Slate*: "The President Is Under FBI Investigation. Is This Normal?"

Every single one of those headlines was a lie. Donald Trump was never the subject of an FBI investigation. You know who was? Hillary Clinton.

The private email server in the basement; deleting more than 30,000 emails from the server *after* a congressional subpoena asking for them; using BleachBit to scrub the emails to render them undetectable—well, to the Establishment media, that's just a big "nothing burger." (More on "nothing burgers" in a minute. Read on!) Evidence? What evidence? Yet, they consider Donald Trump guilty of treason, though there isn't an iota of proof.

Almost everything President Trump does, the Establishment media finds a meandering route to drive it back to Russia.

When the president fired Comey, he did it because Comey was snooping too close to Trump's ties with Russia, and in the days before the termination, Comey asked the Justice Department to put more resources into the investigation. Okay, none of that is true. But that was the narrative the Establishment media pushed around the world:

- *The New York Times*: "Days Before Firing, Comey Asked for More Resources for Russia Inquiry"

- *Washington Post*: "Comey Sought More Resources for Russia Probe Days Before He Was Fired by President Trump, Officials Say"

- *Los Angeles Times*: "Comey Sought More Resources for Russia Investigation Before He Was Fired, Officials Say"

- *Boston Globe*: "Days Before He Was Fired, Comey Asked for Resources for Russia Investigation"

- Reuters: "Comey Had Pushed for More Resources for Russia Probe Before Being Fired by Trump: Source"

- ABC: "Comey Asked for More Money, Staffing for Russia Investigation Days Before Firing"

- CBS: "James Comey Asked DOJ for More Resources for Russia Investigation"

- NBC: "Comey Asked for More Prosecutor Resources for Russia Probe"

- CNN: "Sources: James Comey Sought More Resources for Russia Investigation"

Once again, every one of those headlines was a lie.

In a written statement, deputy attorney general Rod Rosenstein refuted all of it: "I want to address the media claims that the FBI asked for additional resources for the investigation of Russian interference in the 2016 election. I'm not aware of any such request...[I] consulted my staff and

Acting FBI Director Andrew McCabe, and none of them recalls such a request."

Even CNN's Van Jones admitted the Russia/Trump collusion narrative was bogus. Of course, it took a hidden camera sting by Project Veritas to reveal it. On camera, there's Jones stating as plain as the smirk on Putin's face, "the Russia thing is just a big nothing burger." The video came just a couple of days after another Project Veritas video that showed a CNN producer proclaiming the network's Russia stories as ratings-driven "bullsh*t."

Maybe Putin can exile CNN to Siberia where it can exchange the shoveling of crap disguised as news for a season of shoveling snow. At least that's honest labor.

Bogus Russia stories notwithstanding, perhaps the most laugh out loud ludicrous Establishment media moment was something that could be coined, "The Comey/Establishment Flip Flop."

In October 2016, when Comey sent that pesky letter to Congress (the one the moles made him write), the Establishment media and the rest of the demagogues wanted him fired immediately. How dare he cost Hillary votes! But when Comey *was* fired, by President Trump a few months later, he'd been magically transformed into a fighter for justice who'd been wronged by a treasonous president. By the time Comey appeared before the Senate Intelligence Committee a few weeks later, he was now Sir Galahad there to save the day.

It's fun watching the Establishment hypocrisy machine working at full capacity.

Remember when every Establishment television news network and online news website live-broadcasted Hillary Clinton's testimony before the House Select Committee on Benghazi?

Me neither.

But when Comey appeared before the Senate, it was an across the board broadcast spectacular!

"Tune in now to the Comey hearing!"

"Wall to wall coverage of Comey!"

"Click here for the James Comey live feed!"

"Coming up at 5: Comey, Comey, Comey!"

For the Establishment, this was the coup de grâce—the death knell to a president they hate. Comey would prove, with finality, the Establishment ~~obsession~~ contention—that Donald Trump had secret dealings with his Russian BFF, Vladimir Putin, and they colluded to . . . to . . . well, we don't exactly know what they colluded to do, but there was collusion!

Our favorite Establishment media mouthpiece, CNN, trumpeted a story headlined "Comey Expected to Refute Trump" where, using those good ol' reliable anonymous sources, it reported Comey would contradict the president's claims that the FBI director told him he wasn't under investigation. The story was credited to not one but four CNN "journalists," including CNN's chief political analyst, Gloria Borger, who doubled up on the claim, saying on television:

Comey is going to dispute the president on this point if he's asked about it by senators, and we

have to assume that he will be. He will say he
never assured Donald Trump that he was not
under investigation, that that would have been
improper for him to do so.

When Comey's opening statement was released by the Senate Intelligence Committee, Comey did the exact opposite of what CNN reported.

Wowzers!

CNN's story wasn't simply untrue, it was monumentally untrue. Comey provided dates for *three* different times he told the president he wasn't being investigated.

CNN had to change its headline and issue a correction.

Comey, the Establishment's white knight, also outed himself as a serial leaker of the president's memos, but the only thing he seemingly didn't leak was the one thing President Trump asked him to acknowledge—that he was not under investigation.

Comey was nothing more than a disgruntled Obama holdover so peeved at his new boss, he undermined him at every opportunity. The Establishment was praying and hoping he would reveal something, anything, that could lead to impeachment. They promised bombshells. But the ones they hoped would destroy President Trump turned into bombshells that wrecked Comey. He not only revealed himself as a leaker, but also that he was pressured by former attorney general Loretta Lynch to cover for Hillary Clinton by not referring to the investigation of her private email server as an "investigation" but rather as "a matter."

The Establishment spent months spinning the yarn of Russian "collusion," but in the end, the only proven collusion was between Comey and Lynch.

Once the smoke cleared from the Senate hearing, we learned a few incontrovertible things: Donald Trump was never under FBI investigation; he didn't work with Russia to undermine the election; he is not a covert operative for Vladimir Putin; all the reporting by the Establishment media of Russian interference in our election was purposely deceitful; and even MSNBC Establishment shill Chris Matthews knows it's over:

> The assumption of the critics of the president, of his pursuers, you might say, is that somewhere along the line in the last year the president had something to do with colluding with the Russians. Something to do with a helping hand, encouraging them, feeding their desire to affect the election in some way . . . And yet what came apart this morning was that theory.

Conservatism may have beaten the Establishment media this time, but anonymous sources tell CNN, President Trump is conspiring with Dark Lord Sauron for the takeover of Middle Earth.

Stay tuned!

CHAPTER 20

KILLING O'REILLY

For sixteen of the twenty-one years he worked at Fox News, Bill O'Reilly was the untouchable ruler of the cable news kingdom. The show he hosted, *The O'Reilly Factor*, was a ratings juggernaut with more total viewers every day than CNN, MSNBC, CNBC, FBN, or HLN.

Sixteen consecutive years.

Its success was simply unmatched—and that's why the Establishment hated it.

It can't stand that conservative voices resonate so loudly or that they're so popular. Brian Kilmeade said it best when he interviewed actress and liberal loudmouth Janeane Garofalo on *Fox and Friends*. When she accused Fox of having a conservative bias, Kilmeade replied, "Then what does that say about America when it made us number one?" (insert mic drop here)

There's a reason why Rush Limbaugh crushes the ratings of every Establishment voice on the radio. There's a reason why Fox News dominates cable news. And there's a reason *The Factor*, as O'Reilly called it, was without peer.

Conservatives are the voice of America.

The Establishment is the enemy of America.

The Establishment can never beat conservatism on its own merits, so it schemes to subvert it. It sets its sights on the conservatives doing the most damage to their detestable agenda and unleashes a double-barrel blast. The biggest game in the hunt? Bill O'Reilly.

On April Fool's Day 2017, the Establishment's most venerable propagandist, the *New York Times*, published a scathing report that five women who claimed O'Reilly sexually harassed them had been paid a combined $13 million by either Fox or O'Reilly to keep them from pursuing legal action. O'Reilly denied the accusation. What choice did he have if it was without warrant? Someone in a high-profile position dealing with a baseless claim can do one of two things: stand on principle and fight, and hope the ensuing publicity won't destroy their career, or, if you can afford it, pay them to go away—which is what O'Reilly said he did (in a statement posted on his website) for good reason:

> *Just like other prominent and controversial people, I'm vulnerable to lawsuits from individuals who want me to pay them to avoid negative publicity. In my more than 20 years at Fox News Channel, no one has ever filed a complaint about me with the Human Resources Department, even on the anonymous hotline.*
>
> *But most importantly, I'm a father who cares deeply for my children and who would do anything to avoid hurting them in any way. And*

so I have put to rest any controversies to spare
my children.

It's likely no coincidence the *Times* story came out the day after *The O'Reilly Factor* delivered the most-watched quarter in the history of cable television news. It was drawing four million viewers a night. The ratings, in the middle of the fallout from the *Times* story, weren't shrinking—they were actually getting bigger. But company loyalty usually only lasts until it starts costing them money and when advertisers pulled their buys from Fox, that was it—the most successful cable news personality of all time was unceremoniously fired.

That O'Reilly was even more popular in the face of the allegations truly irked the Establishment. Fox planned to ride out the storm. But once they'd decided to cut him, the Establishment scored itself a victory that wasn't in the least bit accidental.

One of O'Reilly's accusers, a woman named Perquita Burgess, was represented by famed publicity hustler Lisa Bloom (remember her from Kathy Griffin's decapitation lovefest?) who, according to the *Washington Post*, told her, "The mission is to bring down Bill O'Reilly."

See, these things don't happen by chance. As O'Reilly's ratings got bigger, to the Establishment, he became more dangerous.

The advertisers that boycotted Fox following news of the harassment claims—like BMW, Mercedes-Benz, Hyundai, Allstate, and other big-money companies—may have been inclined to do so on their own, or may have succumbed to the relentless pressure of a well-financed effort ripped from the Establishment playbook on silencing the opposition.

O'Reilly has been a staunch critic of Establishment-activist billionaire George Soros and his relentless attacks on conservatives through Establishment propaganda groups like Media Matters, which he helps fund. Soros' finances make possible protests against conservatives—the Women's March, Black Lives Matter, Ferguson, Berkeley.

O'Reilly knows companies don't drop advertising on the most-watched cable news show in the world by happenstance. He went on Glenn Beck's radio program and said he was the victim of an organized "hit"—that there's a group that "goes in and terrorizes sponsors, that threatens people behind the scenes, that pays people to say things . . . It has to do with destroying voices that the far left and the organized left-wing cabal doesn't like."

Soros funds those types of groups—groups like Center for Popular Democracy and Make the Road New York. They created a campaign to "name and shame" companies that stand to benefit from President Trump's immigration policies. The groups targeted eight: Goldman Sachs, JPMorgan Chase, Wells Fargo, Blackstone, IBM, Boeing, Uber, and Disney. As *Time* magazine reported, the groups bombard "their elected representatives with letters, calls, and town hall protests to encourage lawmakers to resist President Trump."

These groups don't even try to hide the targeting anymore, as Rashad Robinson of the black activist group, Color of Change, told *Salon*, which reported how when the *Times* story about O'Reilly broke, women's right's group UltraViolet, the

National Organization of Women, Media Matters, and a loose coalition of advertising insiders who call themselves the Sleeping Giants mobilized thousands of people to sign petitions and contact O'Reilly's advertisers to urge them to remove their sponsorships." By the way, Color of Change was co-founded by Van Jones, who, as we mentioned earlier, just happens to be a CNN contributor.

This is a war. The Establishment seeks total decimation of conservatives and the American way of life. Their schemes are well funded, devious, subversive, and, as we saw with O'Reilly, often effective.

They tried it with Fox's Sean Hannity as well. Establishment guerrillas targeted the sponsors of *Hannity* after the show began airing stories on the shooting death of Seth Rich, a DNC staffer some have speculated was the source of embarrassing DNC emails published by WikiLeaks.

The campaign to scare the sponsors failed, due in no small part to Hannity's ubiquitous rants about it on all his media platforms.

O'Reilly told Newsmax he should have fought back the same way Hannity did:

> This was no accident that our sponsors were attacked . . . Hannity knows they're looking to get him, but I admire Sean and how he handled the situation. He brought it directly to the folks, and the sponsors stopped. He lost a few but they stopped so he was successful in fighting off the attack, but there will be more.

Conservatives cannot afford to sit idly by while anti-American forces devour civility and discourse. Freedom and the very fabric of our great nation are at stake. It's a fight for America's soul and everything that makes it exceptional. It's a war the Establishment simply cannot win.

SECTION 6

FINAL THOUGHTS

CHAPTER 21
THE ENEMY WITHIN

My father taught me many things here . . .
He taught me, keep your friends close but
your enemies closer.

–Michael Corleone
The Godfather Part II

For President Trump, following the advice of Michael Corleone shouldn't be difficult. His enemies may be as near as an office down the hall.

There is a deliberate, concerted effort within the federal government to undermine the Trump administration agenda for making America great again. It's commonly referred to as "deep state." Like most of the Establishment's subversion, it's rooted in impeding the president's goals by using underhanded methods like leaking information to an all-to-eager-to-use-it Establishment media.

We've already seen how former FBI director James Comey leaked memos of conversations he had with President Trump to a buddy and asked him to share the contents with the media. The man admitted it in a Senate hearing—talk about ballsy. In fact, Comey was so matter-of-fact about this, the president's former campaign manager, Corey Lewandowski, shredded him in an interview on ABC's *Good Morning America*:

> He is the deep state in Washington that is everything that is wrong. He admitted under oath that he gave his contemporaneous notes to a law professor.

Comey was a bitter Obama appointee who put revenge politics over what should have been his number-one priority—law enforcement. It's so emblematic of the Establishment—politics, driven by hubris, always goes before the good of the country.

The not-so-secret subculture within the government is disdainful of the American people. Its sole aim is simple really—to keep President Trump from implementing the things America put him office to do: lower taxes, repeal Obamacare, rescue business from stifling regulation, strengthen the military, strengthen border security, build the wall, increase jobs . . . you know, make America great again.

Deep state is petulance from the defeated side of a divided nation—divided by an Establishment well aware that division, especially by class and race, leads to socialism.

Establishment media is complicit in the deep state's agenda. It gobbles up leaks from within the government like ravenous lions prowling the Serengeti. Perhaps that's why it doesn't like to acknowledge the deep state even exists. Take this article from the *New Yorker*: "There Is No Deep State: The Problem in Washington Is Not a Conspiracy Against the President; It's the President Himself." Or how about *POLITICO*: "The Deep State Is a Figment of Steve Bannon's Imagination." The article begins with what its writer surely thought was a clever tip for the uneducated:

> *Here's a handy rule for assessing the credibility of what you're reading about national security in the Trump era: If somebody uses the term "Deep State," you can be pretty sure they have no idea what they're talking about.*

Well, that's not quite accurate. It should read more like:

Here's a handy rule for assessing the credibility of what you're reading in the Establishment press or see on an Establishment broadcast in the Trump era: If the reporter uses the phrase "In a leaked report . . ." you can be pretty sure it might not be true and that it certainly came from a deep state operative.

Of course, the Establishment is going to say the deep state doesn't exist—they're the beneficiaries of it. By obtaining information from deep state operatives, they get to delude themselves into believing they're real journalists. But it's comical that in one breath, the Establishment will deny the existence of the deep state and in the other, openly advocate for it.

In June 2017, the American Constitution Society (ACS) held its convention in Washington, DC, where Establishment voices raised up and called for the continued growth of the deep state. As reported by the *Washington Examiner*, a UCLA law professor named Jon Michaels said he "favors filling the Trump administration with liberals opposed to Trump's agenda":

> *We hear a lot of language about draining the swamp and this idea about a deep state that somehow was going to thwart the intentions or the political mandate of the president. I kind of embrace this notion of the "deep state."*

All we heard from the Establishment for the eight years of the Obama administration was how conservatives needed to "reach across the aisle"—that compromise with the president was for the good of the country and those who wouldn't work with him were being petulant. Evidently, compromise only goes one way with the Establishment. The other way? Work from within to destroy the administration.

Senator Mazie Hirono of Hawaii spoke at the ACS convention and called the Trump presidency "a stress test for our country." On that we can agree, although we disagree on the reason why. You think it's him, we know it's you. Hirono's advice for surviving the stress test? "We must work to protect the independence of the federal judiciary and we must ensure that nobody is above the law."

Unless, of course, they're deep state.

CONCLUSION

Many an op-ed has been written about how the Establishment is waging war against Donald Trump. And while that is a fact, we need to understand one other brutal fact of life—the entire country is under attack by the Establishment.

The Establishment hates commonsense governance. It takes job creation, fiscal responsibility, and policies that strengthen our defense and swaps them for political correctness, which is the enemy of America.

The Establishment puts identity politics over the concerns of the hardworking men and women who drive the engine of our economy.

The Establishment laughs at people who embrace morality and decency.

The Establishment infiltrates our schools—from kindergarten to college—indoctrinating young minds with anti-American propaganda.

The Establishment breeds entitled, coddled crybabies who, unable to deal with the realities of life, seek safe spaces.

The Establishment believes life's rewards should be equitable regardless of effort.

The Establishment believes in the power of "free"—especially when it's someone else's dime.

The Establishment vilifies success. It stokes the fire of class envy.

The Establishment is fascism—using violence to silence the voices of those with whom they disagree.

The Establishment misuses the power of the news media—spreading disinformation and shaping narratives in hopes of swaying public opinion into mirroring theirs.

The Establishment is elitism masked as caring.

The Establishment is celebrity activists believing fame entitles them to a bully pulpit.

The Establishment is a belief in the nanny state.

The Establishment is using the media to spread lies in the hopes that the mere appearance of wrongdoing will hurt an intended target.

The Establishment is the effort to overthrow the president of the United States by any means necessary.

The Establishment is the leaking of information for political gain at the risk of national security.

The Establishment sits for the national anthem.

The Establishment is subjecting TV viewers to a lecture on gun control during a football game.

The Establishment believes having pride in your country makes you xenophobic.

The Establishment pushes socialism for others yet embraces the trappings of capitalism for themselves.

The Establishment demands higher taxes and thinks nothing of punishing achievement by taking more of your money.

The Establishment is open borders and un-vetted refugees.

The Establishment is so much more than what's in the pages of this book. But ultimately what the Establishment is . . .

The Establishment is everything opposed to making America great again.

ACKNOWLEDGMENTS

Nick Adams

Tackling a project of this magnitude was challenging and intimidating.

I am grateful to the excellent team at Post Hill Press, whose enthusiasm for this project was infectious and evident from the early stages. Anthony Ziccardi remains an incredible friend and mentor. Our occasional Manhattan lunch or dinner at Italian restaurants are always memorable!

Special mention must be made to the brilliant, creative, and insightful Dave Erickson. Without him, my end product would not be nearly as persuasive or strong. I owe him a beer, or three!

To rising Fox News star and FLAG Advisory Council member Pete Hegseth, who was kind enough to furnish the foreword: you are a patriot of the highest order. Your loyalty and talent are remarkable. It is an honor to call you friend. Thank you.

To my parents: thank you for your unconditional love, unswerving support, and useful advice, solicited and otherwise. (I'm looking at you, Dad!) Once more, when it came to the final stages of this book, my father's steady hand helped.

To Sadie, my special friend: thanks for making life better.

To Sanjay, my best friend: your counsel and conversations sustain me.

To Evan, Ange, Mick, Jimmy, Nick, and Pete: thanks for being wonderful friends for so many years through peaks and valleys.

To my friends, Esteban Blanco and Chris Centineo: thank you for your friendship, always being there for me, and making my transition to life in a new country much easier.

Other people that need mention: Sherrie and Tony McKnight, Don Gobin, Steve Tate, Dianne Edmondson, Robbi Hull, Nam-Yong Horn, Debbie Georgatos, Starr Pitzer, Robert Krueger, Jack Temple, Eddie Taylor, Tommy Melvin, Jeanie Wendt, Jo Miller, Paul Rieger, Shawn Tully, Heather Grier Blanco, Kat Rowoldt, James Graham, John Vobis, Carol Elmore, Linda Stratton, Carlos Stratton, and Jon Stratton.

Most importantly, thanks to Him, from whom all blessings flow.

Dave Erickson

I can honestly say this project was one of the toughest I've had in the whole of my career.

Writing a book is hard, man! Nevertheless, I've wanted to do it for a long time, and thanks to some amazing people, I finally got a shot.

First and foremost, I want to thank God for the desire, the ability, and the opportunity. Without Him I have nothing. Without Him I am nothing.

I can't say enough about the incredible team at Post Hill Press. Michael Wilson—my brother from another mother—and

Anthony Ziccardi took a chance on a first-time author, and never wavered in their belief I could do the job. For giving an unknown like me a shot, I'll be forever grateful. Managing editor Billie Brownell, thank you for putting up with my weekly, "Yeah, I just need another week." It won't happen again. (He's says with a wink and a smile.) Also, our editor, Jon Ford, was phenomenal in helping us tighten and clarify many of the points we wanted to make. Thank you, buddy!

Nick Adams, what can I say? His love of America is an inspiration. He is a true patriot and I can't think of a finer evangelist for the American way of life. I'm so incredibly thankful he allowed me to be a part of this project. Nick also introduced me to this great little Lebanese restaurant in Arlington, Texas. Sure, it's a dump but—It. Is. Awesome!

Rayetta Sanchez, Frank Uribe, Mark Miessner, and Tom Meintzer: thank you for your prayers. You probably have no idea how needed they were. You all are warriors!

Lastly, but as is the cliché, in no way least, I thank four people without whom I couldn't achieve anything.

Thank you to my beautiful daughter, Christina. She is the love of my life, my muse and the reason I get out of bed in the morning. There isn't a day she doesn't inspire me to be the best that I can be and there isn't a day she doesn't make me a proud daddy.

My parents, Maurice and Veronica, by example, taught me the value of setting goals and working hard to achieve them. They came from poor, but proud, hard-working families. They started with nothing yet with a tireless work ethic became successful in every area of life. My parents are the living, breathing embodiment of the American Dream. They've afforded me every opportunity to be successful in life and a man could not ask for two finer people to call "Dad" and "Mom."

My Laurie, what she's meant to me is, well, words can't adequately convey. She's made sacrifice after sacrifice so that I could do this for a living. Laurie was there for me when no one else was. She's supported me. She's pushed me. She's edited me. She's listened to me. Anyone who knows me knows that is no small task. I talk. A lot. Laurie's little notes of encouragement when I wanted to give up in the middle of this oft-frustrating project meant more to me than she probably realizes. She always kept me mindful that this book was for "real" people and not high-minded "look at how smart I am" Establishment types. Laurie, I love you and thank you for believing in me, even when I didn't believe in myself.

Lastly—I'm thankful to be living in the greatest country in the world. No, that does not make me a xenophobe. God bless America covfefe

ABOUT THE AUTHORS

Nick Adams is the Founder and Executive Director of The Foundation for Liberty and American Greatness (FLAG, flagusa.org). He is an internationally known speaker, author, and commentator.

Adams is best known for work in the field of American exceptionalism and is credited with fueling its worldwide resurgence. He contributes to numerous media organizations and has received several awards, including honorary citizenship, as well as being recognized for "extraordinary ability" by the US government.

In addition to this book, Adams is the author of *Retaking America* and *Green Card Warrior*.

Dave Erickson is a satirist, social commentator, award-winning journalist, and Emmy®-winning television producer. He's known for his biting wit and a fearlessness to say what people are thinking but are too afraid to say themselves.

Erickson's Twitter feed (@DaveErickson) and the op-eds on his website have been quoted in the *New York Daily News*, *Mashable*, *Yahoo! News*, *BuzzFeed*, CNN.com, the *Washington Times*, the *Arizona Republic*, and many other sites.

Erickson has appeared on *Dr. Drew On Call*, HLN's *Daily Share*, *On the Case*, *HLN Now*, and Newsmax's *Steve Malzberg Show*.

As a television journalist, Erickson has written, produced, and reported several long-form television investigative series on a broad range of subjects, earning an Associated Press award for his coverage of troop deployments for Operation Desert Storm.

Erickson is a phenomenal dancer, (if you count "the running man") chili chef, musician, and Renaissance man who, when he isn't working, enjoys reading and binge-watching AC/DC videos on YouTube.